T0380927

# THE TALANIAN

# WAY

CHARLES M. TALANIAN

This book is a work of non-fiction. Unless otherwise noted, the author and the publisher make no explicit guarantees as to the accuracy of the information contained in this book and in some cases, names of people and places have been altered to protect their privacy.

Archway Publishing books may be ordered through booksellers or by contacting:

Archway Publishing
1663 Liberty Drive
Bloomington, IN 47403
www.archwaypublishing.com
844-669-3957

Because of the dynamic nature of the Internet, any web addresses or links contained in this book may have changed since publication and may no longer be valid. The views expressed in this work are solely those of the author and do not necessarily reflect the views of the publisher, and the publisher hereby disclaims any responsibility for them.

Any people depicted in stock imagery provided by Getty Images are models, and such images are being used for illustrative purposes only.
Certain stock imagery © Getty Images.

ISBN: 978-1-6657-3380-9 (sc)
ISBN: 978-1-6657-3381-6 (hc)
ISBN: 978-1-6657-3382-3 (e)

Library of Congress Control Number: 2022921696

Print information available on the last page.

Archway Publishing rev. date: 04/12/2023

# DEDICATION

———◆◆◆———

I dedicate this book to the people in my life who gave of themselves to pave the way for a poor immigrant family to build a legacy to the City of Boston, and all the people who visit and tour Back Bay now and in the future.

I would like to thank my grandparents, Azniv and Nishan Semonian, for having the courage to come to America. They always worked hard to build something while at the same time always being kind generous and supportive with an open mind, creating a loving, supportive, and encouraging home for their children and grandchildren.

My mother and father, Nevart and Charles Talanian, were born here, but in their own way were just as brave and loving as my grandparents.

My father fought against all odds to be a better man and provider. Never going to high school or college, coming from nothing, wanting to make a better life for himself and his family, leveraging his smarts, he never shied away from hard work and trusted his instincts and his vision.

My mother, no matter the sacrifice or risk, was a continuous support and sounding board for my father and his ideas. She bravely took on a man who marched to the beat of his very different drum and never questioned his decisions, standing by his side as he made one risky move after another and did back-breaking work for almost unbearable hours.

Thank you dad, for sharing your experiences, your wisdom, and words of advice that to this day are woven into my thinking and replay in my head, guiding me in my own battles and decisions. Your risks, your challenges, your sacrifice, and your dedication and love for your family gave me the platform to build something impactful for the city, the people, our family, and for generations to come that I hope would make you proud.

Finally, to my lovely wife, Ann, who saw the value in sharing our family story and impact with others. Ann gave me the inspiration and ability to jump in and write this book. Thank you for seeing this vision through with me and always offering support and love.

# TABLE OF CONTENTS

# CHAPTER 1
# BEGINNINGS

————◦•◦————

I understand buildings. As strange as it sounds, they speak to me. The pitch of the roofline, the red or cream-colored bricks, the radiators, the old coal furnaces, the mesh of wiring, the pine floors, the square footage, the Sheetrock or paneled walls, and the street on which the property stands—all of these tell me what it would be like to live there or to rent to people or businesses and, most important, given the work I've done for over a half century, the value of the building, the cost of owning it, and the potential profit if I decide to sell.

I suppose this understanding qualifies as one of those mysterious talents. I'm lucky to have it because I always had trouble reading and retaining information and getting the right answers on tests. Not that I didn't work hard (and eventually, I did manage to graduate from college.) But I started school in the 1950s, and while it's now clear that I struggle to read with comprehension, a problem that would plague me on and off into adulthood, back then my teachers considered me intellectually challenged.

During my childhood, I was insatiably curious about mechanical things—how a bicycle worked, for instance, and why a lamp went on when you flicked the switch. In my free time, I enjoyed digging stuff out of the trash and making a variety of things. If I received a toy for my birthday or Christmas, I was far more interested in taking it apart and putting it together again than I was in playing with it. Later on, I began tinkering with hammers, nails, and wood and built forts and tree houses. And as frustrated as I was in school, I learned that there was a place for people like me in the world.

My father's brother-in-law, James Mukjian, was a physics professor at Northeastern University who also contracted with the government to do work at the Charlestown Navy Yard. He wore bow ties and tweed sport coats, and he was evidently quite intelligent. One day, I stopped by his house, and he was having a problem. He had just bought a stereo with all the latest components. He had plugged the speakers into the receiver along with the AM/FM radio and a turntable on top. He was sitting there reading the directions and scratching his head because when he put down the tone arm, the needle would skid across the record. My first instinct was to pick up the arm, which I did, and I saw that the plastic protector was still on the needle. So I snapped it off, dropped the arm, and the music played. For Jim, if it wasn't written in the directions, he couldn't figure it out. That was when I realized the difference between a learned man and a handy man.

My parents never gave me any stern lectures about my performance in school. In part, it was because they knew I was trying, and they were the opposite of today's helicopter parents. In addition, I believe their acceptance of my situation was because my father shared a dislike of book learning and a love for all things mechanical. My mother, Nevart Semonian, realized it soon after she met Charles Talanian at an Armenian church picnic in the summer of 1940. Nevart had grown up in West Somerville; Charles had been born in Cranston, Rhode Island. I'm told that my father was an excellent dancer. Whether this was the deciding factor for my mother accepting his proposal, I can't say. They were married in 1941.

At the time, Charles was operating a grocery store in West Roxbury. He closed the store when the Second World War began and joined the Army Air Corps. He applied to become an airplane mechanic and lied about his education. On the application, he used his brother's credentials from high school and college. He was assigned to Laurence G. Hanscom Field in Bedford, Massachusetts. One afternoon, he was reading a book about how to repair airplane wings when a colonel called him aside and informed him that he had been caught: he didn't have the education he'd claimed, and he had been faking it on the job.

"You're right," he told the colonel. "But let me take the mechanic's test. It can't be written. Just give me a verbal test and a blackboard. I'll show you I can do the work."

His request was granted, and Charles passed the test.

He used to fly in the planes with the test pilots because one of the crucial projects he was assigned was to stabilize the cameras that took the pictures used for bomb-damage assessment. The Army Air Corps was having trouble making the cameras hold still, and Charles, along with the Bendix Spring Company, figured out how to mount the cameras so they wouldn't vibrate. The planes weren't heated in those days, and I remember, as a child, seeing the sheep-lined leather gloves he used to wear on those flights. I still have the two toolboxes that he had custom-made with wheels on them. Whenever a mechanic needed a tool, he had to walk all the way back to the hanger and then return to the plane on the tarmac. It was a waste of time. But with wheels on the boxes, the tools would be right at hand. No one suggested the idea to Charles. It just made sense.

After the war ended, Charles opened a Kaiser-Fraiser automobile dealership and garage. This was a logical choice given his mechanical ability. It was there that he learned how to sell and keep clients happy. He used to tell the story of the couple who came in one day. They were not particularly well-dressed, and they spoke broken English. None of the salesmen got up to assist them but my father did, and wouldn't you know the couple paid cash for a new car, annoying the salesmen and underscoring for my father what he believed: that you never really know about strangers. So it's a good policy to give them the benefit of the doubt and treat them with respect.

It wasn't long before my father bought his first house and, shortly thereafter, discovered a whole new career.

Around that time, I came along, on June 3, 1946, to be exact, and throughout my early years, I watched my father as he founded and maintained the C. Talanian Realty Company. He used to say that if you're a surgeon, you're working with your hands. Sure, you might make good money, but if something happens to your hands, you're in trouble. You have to work with your brain. That's the last thing to go."

Working with his brain meant buying and managing properties, and his advice and career choice made a huge impression on me. In the summers, if my father was doing repairs on his buildings, I'd work for him, sweeping floors, steaming wallpaper, pulling nails out of two-by-fours to be reused, and learning how to fix things. After college, I needed a job and scoured the want ads in the newspapers. I interviewed twice to be an aide for a handicapped professor at Woods Hole Oceanographic Institute, but I didn't get that one. My father suggested that I look in the newspapers at his office. I went over, and he mentioned that he and my mother were going to Florida for a week's vacation and I could handle any checks that needed to be signed or any repairs that came up.

I wanted to help out my parents, and before I knew it, I was fielding complaints from his tenants on the phone. I had a toolbox in my car and drove around to fix the problems.

This was my beginning in the real estate business. And when I decided to tell my story, I saw that I was, in fact, telling stories of the buildings that my father, and then I, had purchased. They are tied to the most important moments of my life: my marriage, the birth of my son, the illness and death of my wife, and my remarriage.

I see my history in those buildings. They do talk to me, and now, I hope you can a hear a little bit of what I hear. And they will speak to you as well.

# CHAPTER 2
# EDEN ON WHITTEN STREET

The first building that my parents owned in Boston was a modest two-family house at 38 Whitten Street in what is now known as the St. Mark's section of Dorchester. My father purchased the property in 1943. The house was chocolate-brown with white trim, and he paid $3,000 or $4,000. My parents, I'm told, didn't have the $400 needed for the down payment, but the seller liked my dad and they worked out a deal where he paid off the money over a period of months.

Like a lot of families at that time, my uncle, my father's brother, Albert, and his wife, Ann, shared the house with us. They lived in the downstairs apartment, and we occupied the second floor, two bedrooms, a living room, dining room, kitchen, and an attic. The insulation was terrible, and Dad used to install heavy, wooden, storm windows that would ice up in the winter. My mother cooked on a wood-burning stove that had been converted to kerosene, and the bathroom featured a cast-iron bathtub with legs and a water closet with a toilet you flushed by tugging a long chain hanging from the ceiling. After my father's youngest sister, Virginia, married, she and her husband, Michael, moved into the attic. Half of the attic was storage space, and the livable part followed the roofline so it was low and cramped. I shared the bedroom off the kitchen with my older sister, Gail, until I was two or three years old, which was when Aunt Virginia and Uncle Mike found a place of their own, and Gail moved up to the attic.

The Dorchester I recall was a blue-collar neighborhood full of two-family houses. It was a great time for the middle class. The war was over; returning veterans were getting new jobs, marrying, starting families, and buying homes. We kids could play safely in the streets. My father had a car, but he was the exception. Mainly, adults walked everywhere or took the train. Children were given a lot of freedom if we stayed on our block. We just had to be home before dusk, which was when a city worker came along to light the gas streetlamps. I remember the ragman riding in on his horse-drawn wagon to collect rags, the older fellow who came through to sharpen knives and scissors, the milkman putting the sweating milk bottles in the metal box on our back porch, and the iceman delivering the ice that was stored in big, wooden, insulated chests. Reliable freezers and refrigerators didn't become affordable for the middle class until the mid-1950s. Our freezer could barely make a tray of ice cubes, and this explains why I have an indelible memory of people always going out for ice cream—whether to the truck that stopped in the neighborhood or heading down the block to a store.

In those days, Boston was a factory town, which is hard to imagine now that the factories are gone, the city has such a dazzling skyline, and the neighborhoods have skyrocketed in value. In Dorchester, there was the Baker's Chocolate Factory, a complex of redbrick buildings along the Neponset River dating back to the 1800s. The factory shut down in the 1960s and met the not unusual fate of buildings from the industrial past: it was transformed into condominiums. Growing up in Dorchester, you knew it was going to rain if you could smell the chocolate because the wind picked up. The rich fragrance was a constant presence in the summer because without air-conditioning the windows stayed open. The

Baker's chocolate bars had a lady with a hat and long dress printed on them, and I'll never forget how wonderful the chocolate tasted.

There was a Catholic nursing home behind our house, and on summer nights, you would hear, through our screened windows, the residents saying their prayers. One benefit of living behind a nursing home was that deliveries were made in the back of the building that abutted the backyards of our house and the houses of our neighbors, and when the Wonder Bread truck arrived, the driver would see us and hand out cupcakes. When the milk truck showed up, that driver proved to be equally generous when he noticed the kids hanging on the fence; he gave us a quart of chocolate milk to share. Today such treats might seem modest, but to us they were gestures of incredible kindness, and it was only later that I realized the drivers had probably paid for their donations out of their pockets. The worst thing we children did was when the garbage man drove his truck behind the nursing home to pick up the trash. He didn't have anything to give us, so we used to hide behind a tree and shout, "Hello, Stinky!"

Interestingly enough, as a child, my career goal was to become a garbage man. I thought their knitted skullcaps were cool, and the men rode on the back of the truck before jumping off to collect trash. I mean, come on! What could be better than that? It was as if they spent all day on an amusement park ride. My mother even knit me one of those skullcaps that the garbage men wore. To me, that was the good life.

My father had other ideas about work and what made for a suitable career. Dad was always out on a job or at his office so we didn't spend a lot of time together, but I remember him telling me that working with your hands would eventually prove to be more difficult as you got older. That was why he entered the real estate business. It was a brave decision, particularly for someone who had grown up during the Great Depression and was raised with the mindset of securing a job with a weekly paycheck from a company that promised a pension to take care of you after retirement. To work for yourself put all the pressure on you, and it wasn't for everyone. The newfound financial security people were enjoying amid the postwar American economy was something to safeguard, not risk.

Yet my father believed in risk, the freedom that accompanied it, and the promises of a bigger profit. He secured a builder's license in Boston and Cambridge and worked as a real estate broker for Tom Diab in the 1950s. Diab owned numerous properties, and his office was at 52 Beacon Street. Diab would buy real estate anywhere in New England, and he did property management and provided mortgages to buyers. He had a lot of money to spread around, and he was doing condominium conversions before anybody really knew what those were. Several of his properties were vacant, and my father suggested that they put a coat of paint on the buildings and rent them out until Diab was ready to remodel them. Diab agreed. I was very young at that time and, along with a ruler I had with Diab's name on it that were handed out to customers, I remember they were buying places in Cohasset such as a pig farm estate. The five-car garage became a condominium, and the main home became four more. Diab bought the R. H. Stern building on Tremont Street, right across from Park Street Station. It had been a department store in the 1950s, and I recall being with Dad while an area was being gutted. He found a plastic box of Christmas decorations and gave it to me. That building still has the glass and steel awning over the front door.

Diab and Dad undertook similar projects in St. Petersburg, Florida, and Diab was supposed to take in my father as a partner on two or three deals but double-crossed him at the last second. My father was proud that he always kept his word and disliked dealing with people who didn't. He also felt that he had been doing an excellent job for Diab managing his buildings, and if he had no future with Diab, he was better off going out on his own. So he did.

Still, as busy as he was, Dad made sure that he taught me the value of hard work, and I mean hard, physical labor. When I was old enough, he paid me a weekly allowance of ten cents for taking out the ash barrels. Houses had coal-burning furnaces, which is why the little windows at the foundation are known as coal-chute windows. The windows were used to deliver coal into the wooden bins in the basement by the furnace. Our house had two coal-chute windows: one for my father's furnace and the other for my uncle's. The coal was fed into separate bins, with wood slats separating the layers. When the coal was piled up, you shoveled it from the top down to the bottom. Dad shoveled the coal into the furnace. That was relatively easy compared to what came next: cleaning out the furnaces by shoveling the ashes into corrugated metal barrels.

Talk about a tough job! I was maybe three-feet tall then, and the ash-filled barrel was very heavy. Getting it from the basement to the curb felt like moving a boulder. I had to navigate three steps up from the basement to get to a side door and another three steps down to the sidewalk in front of the house. I learned that it was easiest to carry the ash barrel the whole way up from the basement and outside to the curb without stopping and having to lift the barrel up again. And I had to be careful. I vividly recall three occasions as I hustled to carry the ash barrel to the street when I made the mistake of dropping the barrel hard on the ground instead of carefully setting it on the curb. The extra force sent up a puff of ash, and the ashes went into my eyes. I felt as though someone had poked tiny razor blades into my pupils. My mother would have to take me to the doctor when that happened so he could wash the ashes out of my eyes. Eventually, I'm happy to report, those coal-fired, asbestos furnaces were converted to oil fuel. They would put an oil tank in where the coal bin was, run a copper line, and put an oil-fired gun at the bottom of it. Converting to oil was stepping up in class.

Those days are long gone. Now I sit in one of my homes in Boston, Florida, or Cape Cod and remember the simple pleasures of that era. My family didn't have much, and I wonder if it would have been easier for me to crash and burn had I been born closer to the top rung. Perhaps. But I tend, while taking a risk, to be very careful, to avoid looking for the fast score or the easy money. Most of all, my childhood imbued me with the values ones needs to succeed: a willingness to take rational chances and a commitment to work, no matter how many hours, until you get to where you want to go.

When those days come back to me, one feeling overrides all the others: I feel blessed.

# CHAPTER 3
# FINDING A VOCATION

By the time I was nine years old, I was using a blowtorch to heat floor tiles for my father. All my friends were playing football, baseball, and hide-and-seek, but I wouldn't have traded places with them for love or money. Are you kidding? A blowtorch! I thought it was coolest instrument in the world.

At first, how this opportunity came my way was a mystery. Every Sunday, my sister and I would go around the corner to the church on Dick Street in Dorchester for Sunday school. When we got home, we would get in the car with my parents and drive into Boston to an Armenian church on Shawmut Avenue. When the service was over, my parents would drive around the suburbs and look at houses. Gail and I didn't catch on. Despite going to two Sunday schools and two churches every Sunday and then looking at houses for the rest of the day, we didn't realize that our parents were anxious to leave Dorchester.

This was our Sunday family routine for two years. My father was trying to find the right place to live. By nature, Dad was careful, thinking through every important decision from top to bottom, especially when it came to real estate. The property not only had to be the proper place for his family but also worth the money and a wise, long-term investment. There was a development up on Belmont Hill, off Marsh Street, near the Belmont Hill School. The subdivision was called Hillcrest. My parents ended up buying a lot there. I suspect Dad wondered why he should buy a house when he was capable of building one of his own, both saving money and winding up with the home that he and Mother wanted. He built a modest ranch house on Stony Brook Road, and we moved there in 1956, shortly before my tenth birthday. The streets were unpaved, and there were empty lots as far as I could see. We were among the earliest families to move in. It was a good choice. Eventually, Belmont would become one of the most upscale suburbs of Boston.

I remember the first time I went there with Dad. The foundation had just been poured. On our next visit, the flooring had been installed. And then on another Sunday, I saw that a load of lumber had been dropped off in the front yard. My father told me that he received the first load for free from a lumber yard in Cambridge. He bought all of his lumber there for his remodeling jobs, and they gave him a load for free to thank him for being such a good customer over the years.

I remember my father going to the house with his cousin and brother-in-law to pick up the lumber from the front yard and take it to the backyard so that no one would steal it. They figured that someone might be able to back up their truck to the lumber and steal if it was in the front of the house but it would be safe in back. Of course, this wasn't true. Thieves generally aren't that picky. They'll steal from the back or the front. But evidently Belmont wasn't a high-crime area because not one piece of lumber ever went missing.

I would go every weekend with my father so he could check on the progress of the construction. It didn't bother me at all not playing with my friends. I enjoyed watching the house going up piece by piece. I saw the foundation being poured, and when the wooden forms were removed, there were still the steel rods, side by side, going right through the cement. This was the first job that my father gave me. I had to put a four-foot length of pipe on the steel rod, bend it to the right, and then bend it to the left to break them off. I recall thinking that I was going to be paid a buck for my work.

When the house was finished, it was almost 2,500 square feet, including the basement, which wasn't like basements in Dorchester, packed with pipes, wires, coal furnaces, and boilers. In our house, the basement served as a playroom. Sure, there were utilities, storage, a hot water heater, and a washer-and-dryer, but it was also used for parties, and we would celebrate Christmas down there.

We installed a cedar closet in the basement—a closet used to protect coats and wool clothing from moths—and we put a safe in the closet. Before we installed the safe, it was sitting on the basement floor. I started playing with it and managed—don't ask me how—to open it. After we installed it, I was the only person in the house who could open the safe for my mother and father. I had a deep connection to that house and everything about it. I was very inquisitive.

Now for the blowtorch. Dad didn't want to hire someone to lay the tile in the basement. Part of the reason may have been he didn't want to spend the money, but most of it was that he wanted it done perfectly. The tiles happened to be very brittle, and they had to be heated until softened so if the floor wasn't plumb, the tiles would bend to the curves. I heated the tiles then handed them to my father, and he would lay them down.

It seems straightforward enough, and even as a child I didn't give it a second thought. However, in retrospect, I believe my father had more in mind than simply spending a few hours with his young son.

My trouble reading made school a misery. I didn't dislike my teachers or my classmates, but no matter how hard I tried, my grades were terrible. My parents saw that I put in the time with my homework so they never scolded me for my poor report cards. In Belmont, I attended Burbank School and Belmont Junior High, and when my grades didn't improve, I was sent to boarding school at Laurel Crest Academy in Bristol, Connecticut, where academic success still eluded me. I discovered that, unlike my schoolmates, I didn't own a high-fashion wardrobe, and the best place to ski during winter recess was a place I'd never heard of: Gstaad, Switzerland.

Yet my parents believed I needed to have a college degree, so I started out at Belknap College in Center Harbor, New Hampshire. My grades weren't very good, and I tried to transfer to another school in the same state, Nathaniel Hawthorne College. I was accepted there, but when they got a firsthand look at my struggle with the written word, they determined I was stupid and rejected me. So off I went to Parsons College in Fairfield, Iowa, where the teachers were quite kind and helpful. In 1969, after five years, I earned a degree.

From my boyhood on, I believe my father understood that school would be hard for me, and if I'd make anything of myself, it would be using my mechanical skills combined with hard work. I suspect that he shared some of my problems and things had worked out fine for him, which explains why he let a nine-year-old boy use a blowtorch.

Dad was intent on teaching me the lessons he believed I'd need to know, yet I must confess they didn't always make sense to me.

I had a cousin who lived near us in Lexington. He'd had polio as a child; it was difficult for him to get around, and his parents had bought him a little gas car. By the time we moved to Belmont, my cousin wanted to sell the car for $100. There were many dirt roads circling our house where I could ride such a car, and I asked my father if he'd buy it for me.

"You earn half," Dad replied. "And I'll give you the other half."

No one had started a paper route in our development, so I decided that would be my job. I went out and signed up customers. I carried the morning, evening, and Sunday papers through rain, sleet, snow, and the summer heat. I also armed myself with dog biscuits because on occasion I'd have to hand one out to avoid getting bitten by the more territorial dogs in the neighborhood. On my best week, I made $2.35, and it took me over a year to save up $50. I told my father I was ready, and he told me I should call up my cousin and offer him $50 for the car.

That's what I did, but my cousin refused to budge from the $100 price. I informed my father, who thought about it for a moment and then said, "It's not worth a hundred." He didn't give me the money.

I was disappointed, and my feelings were hurt. Wasn't a deal supposed to be a deal? Evidently, sometimes not. I have no idea why Dad changed his mind. Even so, I have to admit that, given my eventual career in real estate, it was a worthwhile lesson, but it hurt like hell to learn it.

# CHAPTER 4
# SAILING INTO BACK BAY

—•◆•—

One Sunday afternoon in the mid-1950s, my family was driving through Boston. My father was at the wheel, my mother next to him, and my sister Gail and I were in the back seat.

As we rode down Commonwealth Avenue, past the intersection of Mass Avenue, Dad said, "I read in the *Globe* that Prudential Life Insurance is going put up a tower near here. When an insurance company puts up a skyscraper, the neighborhood gets better. I'm going to start looking to buy in Back Bay."

Back Bay was created by filling in part of the Charles River Basin. It boasted lovely examples of Victorian brownstones and some notable landmarks—for example, the Boston Public Library—but few real estate people were interested in gambling on the promise of urban renewal and didn't consider the area a smart investment opportunity. The attitude in the 1950s was that the suburbs were place to be; you were cuckoo if you wanted to live in the city and not own a car; and in the parking lots behind the buildings in Back Bay, you saw clotheslines and delivery trucks, not cars. Prudential was building its tower on thirty-one acres from a freight yard, a church, and by knocking down the old Mechanics Hall.

My father was working long hours as a broker and remodeler. I rarely saw him. The summer I was seven, I spent a month at Camp Good News on Cape Cod, and my aunt and uncle had to visit on Parents' Day because Dad was in the hospital after severely cutting his leg on a broken porcelain tub. Financially, my father was keeping his head above water, but he had no investment capital when, one day after leaving his office, he discovered that the apartment building at 232 Newbury Street was for sale. Back then, this was just a sleepy neighborhood and everyone thought if you rented, you rented to students, which wasn't my father's plan. He believed that you were better off renting to tenants who earned their own money, who would appreciate their apartment, and who would take care of it because they—and not their parents—were paying the rent.

At the time, many of the old, exquisite townhouses in Back Bay had seen better days when the people who lived in them could afford them and the servants who catered to their every need. Their heirs were not so fortunate, and they had to rent out rooms to make ends meet. The price of the 232 Newbury house was $20,000. Dad went to talk to his father-in-law, my maternal grandfather. His name was Nishan Simonian. I always called him Dede, Armenian for Grandpa. Along with his brother, Dede owned the Fresh Pond Market on Huron Avenue in Cambridge. He agreed to lend my father $5,000 for the down payment and, seeing that Dad was nervous about the size of his investment, comforted him by saying, "What are you worried about? I own a grocery store and have a big house. So you and your family will always have food to eat and somewhere to live."

I knew my grandfather quite well. He lived until the age of ninety-seven, and he certainly deserved his longevity. He was a very kind man, and even years after he was gone, I still heard stories from people who knew and loved him. I don't know what work Dede did in the old country, but he arrived in the

United States with enough money to buy a two-family house in Somerville, where my mother grew up, and to buy the block of stores and open Fresh Pond Market.

When it came to helping me, his assistance was packaged with a test and a lesson. When I graduated from college, I needed a car, and he lent me $4,000 to buy one. There were no repayment terms, but Dede made it clear that it was a loan. It took me a while to save up to pay him back. When I brought him the check, he wouldn't take it.

"I just wanted to see if you would repay me," he said. "You should always pay your debts."

I often visited my grandfather, and when my parents were away in Florida, I ate dinner with him once a week. He was not formally educated, but he was wise and used to pass along his wisdom via stories. By the time Dede was very old, he'd tell me the same stories over and over again, and I'd pretend that I hadn't heard them, and whenever he laughed, I'd laugh. However, there was one story he'd repeat that I never understood—at least not until many years later when I had accumulated acreage on Cape Cod and had to fight with the Cape Cod Commission about zoning. I'll leave the particulars for later, but my grandfather's story is enlightening for anyone who has battled with the illogically unpersuadable.

"There were two men strolling along a beach," my grandfather said. "One of them points toward a high sand dune, saying, 'Look up there. It's an eagle.' The other man says, 'No, it's a goat.' They argue back and forth until one man says, 'I'm gonna take my slingshot and shoot a rock up there. If it walks away, it's a goat. If it flies away, it's an eagle.' They agree, and the man shoots the rock. The animal moves right and left, and then spreads its wings and flies away. The man says, 'See, I told you. It's an eagle.' And the other man replies, 'No, it's a goat.' " My grandfather never failed to get a kick out of that story. And I'm sure it pleased him to teach me something that I would need to know.

On Saturdays, I accompanied my father to 232. I remember how the tenants would greet him at the door with a respectful and appreciative "Hello, Mr. Talanian."

I watched him do repairs, assisting him when I could. I was fascinated by one aspect of his remodeling business. In the process of converting townhouses into apartments, he often paid for some of it by selling off the antiques—marble pool tables, for instance, or fireplace mantles.

There were nine apartments in 232, and the front of the basement was the boiler room. One special feature of the building was that each apartment had two sets of doors. The outer door was louvered, and the inner door was solid. They were made this way before air-conditioning so you could be in your apartment with your windows and door open but still have the privacy of the louvered door, with air flowing from front to back.

Rent in those days was $20 or $25 a month, so Dad was taking in $5,000 or $6,000 a year. Out of that he had to pay the mortgage, taxes, the janitor, public-hallway electricity, water, fuel, and insurance. There wasn't a lot of money to be made when all was said and done—maybe $150 a year. And he wanted to be fair to his tenants. When he'd go through the rentals to renew the leases, he'd say, "I'm not gonna raise this person twenty cents a month. They're by themselves and they've got a job. I'll only raise them ten cents."

At first, I didn't understand why my father bought 232. Certainly not to fatten his savings account; he had almost nothing socked away. I remember him looking at his mortgage statement from the bank at the end of the year. He saw his savings account as the difference between the amount remaining on the mortgage and the value of the building. He used to tap the statement with his finger and say, "My money is in those bricks."

Even though few investors agreed with his vision—that Back Bay would become valuable—my father kept marching to the beat of his own drum. And his plan was simple. All you had to do was the proper maintenance on your property and have faith in the future. Dad had so much faith that he started looking for other buildings, and within a few years, he had enough capital and net value to expand his holdings.

In 1950, my father bought 320 Commonwealth Avenue and transformed it into nine apartments. While 232 Newbury was still an original apartment building, this was his first major renovation. On the weekends, Dad brought me in and had me working with the laborer, sweeping and shoveling the debris into a dumpster. During the final cleanup, I remember the laborer was down on his hands and knees and scrubbing the bathroom floor. There wasn't enough space in there for me to give him a hand. While I was watching him, he glanced over his shoulder and said to me, "You know there's an easy way of doing this."

I got excited and said, "Yeah? What is it?"

And he said, "This is it."

I always treasured his comment as a gilded slice of wisdom: there are no shortcuts to renovating a property or, for that matter, doing anything worthwhile.

In 1972, when I was working for my father full-time, most of my efforts were basic repairs, and I got a call from the top-floor front tenants. It was springtime, and they wanted me to put in their window screens. Their two-bedroom was up four flights of stairs, and the screens were stored in a closet in the basement. I went to the apartment with my master key and knocked on the door. No one answered. I opened the door and yelled, "Hello! Hello! Is anybody here?"

Again, there was no answer so I entered and looked the situation over—how many windows and what size of screen I'd need. I went to the basement, brought the screens upstairs, and installed them in the windows.

As I was locking their door, two policemen showed up and asked me what I was doing. It turned out that the two people occupying that apartment were stewardesses who would go in and out at strange hours. They each had a bell on their keychain so the woman across the hall, if she heard the bell, knew it was them. Well, she wasn't hearing any bells while I was entering and exiting the apartment, and she phoned the police.

A good neighbor, I suppose, but it unnerved me until I was able to explain my presence to the policemen.

# CHAPTER 5
# TENANTS: LEARNING THE BUSINESS

———◆———

In 1962, Dad bought 39 Fairfield Street. The center stair entrance was on Fairfield, and he renovated the basement and first floor, where a dentist had an office. He put the entrances to the basement and first floor on Newbury Street, then changed the address to 240A Newbury because he thought that one day Newbury would have more prestige and thus more value than Fairfield.

There was little retail on Newbury then so it didn't really mean anything for a store to be located there. My father, however, saw Newbury as a shopping district, or at least he hoped it would be. Until this point, he was still renovating to rent. Condos and co-ops weren't part of our vocabulary until the 1980s. When condos started in Boston, you could buy one for $75 a square foot—an unimaginably low price compared to what was to come. So the majority of landlords who bought in Back Bay kept the buildings for income property. My father believed condos had a future, and he dipped his toe into the market. His most profitable insight was that Newbury Street had a future as a glittering retail street similar to Fifth Avenue in New York City.

Dad had some rules about renting to businesses. "No food, no booze, no hair salons. They're too risky."

Even so, in the winter of 1970, when I had been working for C. Talanian Realty for a year, my parents went to vacation in Florida. On a Sunday, I was sweeping the basement at 240A Newbury Street, and in walked three guys. The oldest one was wearing an overcoat, a scarf, and a hat, and I recognized him as Patrick J. "Sonny" McDonough, speaker of the Massachusetts House of Representatives. Sonny was with his son, Jimmy, and Joe Cimino, both of whom had recently graduated from law school.

I looked up, and Sonny said, "How much?"

Still sweeping, I replied, "Ten dollars a square foot."

Sonny wanted to open a pub. At that time, I was going to New York on a regular basis, and it seemed that I saw pubs on almost every corner. All Boston had was Lucifer's in Kenmore Square. You paid twenty bucks to get in and have lousy drinks in tiny juice glasses. What Sonny described sounded far better.

I phoned my father and explained the offer, saying that I thought we should do it. My father had final say on all deals, but to his credit, he didn't engage in father-knows-best battles with me. He trusted my judgment, figuring that his twenty-four-year-old son would know more about the bar scene than he did.

Dad agreed with me, and a deposit check arrived for $1,000. It had been written by the hockey player Derek Sanderson, who was going to be a partner in the pub. This was the first deal I did on my own.

The pub, Daisy Buchanan's, opened in 1972 and became very successful. Joe Cimino ran it. No food, just booze, rocking, and rolling. Sonny wanted the place paneled with mahogany Statehouse doors that were so thick the carpenters had trouble sawing them to fit. The first floor of the building had a nice double-door entrance on Fairfield Street and an awning where my father wanted to move his real estate office. We still had a door from the other side on Newbury Street, but he wanted to use that entrance to go to the first floor. Dad had already ordered drapes and a chandelier for the conference room, when along came Tech HiFi.

In those days, if you wanted a stereo, you went to Lechmere's to buy a simple stereo and turntable. Tech HiFi was one of the first stores that sold sophisticated stereo equipment. They were willing to pay $10 to $12 per square foot. My father looked at me and asked, "What do you think?"

I said, "Let's take the money. Stay where we are. We are fine."

I'm glad he listened to me. We rented it to Tech HiFi and they were our tenant for ten or fifteen years. When they left, Joe Cimino, who was still managing Daisy Buchanan's in the basement, said, "I'd like to rent the upstairs and put in a restaurant."

I told him, "To put in a restaurant, you'll have to rent the upstairs apartments as well. I can't keep four apartments happy above a restaurant with the noise and the smells from the kitchen."

I ended up triple-net leasing him the entire building. (A triple-net lease means whoever leases the property handles all associated expenses, including taxes.) It turned out to be a great deal for us and for Joe. He opened Ciao Bella, and his sister ran it.

Eventually, C. Talanian Realty became known for digging up basements and making retail space out of them. My father's reason for doing this was not only a result of his vision. The fact is it was less expensive to build a store with no kitchens and one bathroom than keep up two kitchens, two bathrooms, and two apartments. Profit was all about how much you could charge for the square footage, and businesses paid more. In addition, you received a check every month, and you didn't receive frantic calls to fix an oven, window cord, or drippy faucet.

I don't want to exaggerate the problems dealing with tenants. The majority of them are a delight, pay on time, and are not overly demanding. However, I had an experience with one of the tenants at 240A Newbury Street that I can only describe as surreal.

There were four small apartments upstairs, which had electric heat. One of the tenants who had been with us for five years was a prim and proper woman who worked at the C. B. Swift Furniture Company on Newbury Street. One day in the summer, I was driving home and saw her on the sidewalk. She was wearing one of those aprons that goes over the top of your head and covers your front and back. From what I could see, she had no underwear under her apron. I was thinking, *Uh oh. She's gone looney.*

Not long after that, she called me and said that her stove didn't work. I called the repair guy to take care of it, but when he got back to me, he said that there was nothing wrong with the stove.

The tenant called me again. Now her stove didn't work. It was a one-piece oven and stove, and I said, "OK. I'll check it out."

As I walked into her apartment, I saw fall leaves on her table and brown paper bags with all kinds of gibberish written on them. I turned on the four burners of her electric stove, and slowly they became red hot.

She said, "Well, it doesn't boil water."

And I said, "Let me have your kettle."

She handed me the kettle. I filled it with water, put it on a burner, and as the water started to boil, she turned off the switch and said, "I don't want to burn the bottom of my kettle."

I looked at her without knowing exactly what to do as I'm not a psychiatrist, and she asked, "Whose air-conditioning am I hooked up to?"

"There is no air-conditioning in this apartment," I answered.

Then she told me, "You know when I moved in and I'd open the door and the window, and the air would go out. Now I open the window and the air comes in. What's going on with that?"

I calmly tried to explain that I didn't know and left. Needless to say, it got to a point to where she wasn't paying her rent and I had to begin an eviction proceeding against her, always an annoying and heartbreaking undertaking. This meant that I had to take her to housing court, where I'd gone before for rent collections, but eviction is a whole other story.

Luckily there was this very intelligent woman who worked in the courthouse. She owned a three-decker and knew the trials and tribulations of being a landlord. We got to know each other over time, and we were on good terms. She knew I'd never jump to evict someone but would call and try to work out a payment schedule, which was how Dad invariably handled this problem, even though he was operating on such a slim margin that nonpayment of rent really stung.

Anyway, this woman was questioning my tenant, who had complained that she didn't feel well in the apartment. The woman asked her if she thought Mr. Talanian might be putting something under her door that caused her problem.

And my tenant said, "Yes, could be."

I ended up being allowed to evict her. I put her belongings in the basement of another building, and when the winter rolled around, the woman from the court called me and asked, "Do you have any of her stuff? Winter's coming, and she says she doesn't have a coat."

I said, "Tell her I'll give her whatever she wants."

Legally it can take six to nine months to evict a residential tenant. You don't collect rent for those months and have to put their property in storage under their name and prepay for six months so they can collect their things.

We've had plenty of these cases. I often felt terrible for people who were down on their luck and tried my best to keep them in their apartment, and my efforts often paid off for me and my tenants.

However, what I found infuriating were the tenants who gamed the system, knew the law was on their side, and did their best to live rent free.

# CHAPTER 6
# THE SHAKEDOWN

In the early 1960s, my father bought an entire block of buildings in Lynn, Massachusetts, a city that is about ten miles outside of Boston. Among the buildings were a movie theater, a jewelry store, and a sandwich shop. I was in high school and most interested in the theater, where I assumed I'd soon be working as an usher and eating free popcorn.

I don't know why my father bought this particular property. He certainly wasn't familiar with the Lynn real estate market. I'm guessing that he thought he was getting a good deal, that the rents would cover the mortgage, taxes, and upkeep, and that in the end, he'd turn a profit.

That wasn't how it worked out. I recall him saying, "It's too much property. And it's not making enough money."

One approach to correct that problem was to reduce expenses by applying for a tax abatement. My father went to the city assessor and asked for the abatement. He was floored by the answer.

The assessor told him no problem; he could have his tax abatement. Dad just had to give the assessor $25,000 in cash. That was an awful lot of money in those days. You could buy a brick house in a nice suburb for $50,000. Of course, my father didn't have that kind of money sitting around, so he begged and borrowed and finally managed to give the assessor his payoff. The assessment was lowered.

Given how appalled my father was by the shakedown, I suspect this was his first experience with this type of shady dealing. And I suppose, sixty years ago, it was not uncommon. Today, it would be a good way for an assessor to wind up in jail, and in my dealings with assessors, I have my attorneys and chief operating officer handle all the due diligence and number crunching. My job is to supply the vision; I'm the A to Z guy. I don't do the L-M-N-O-P.

Several years after turning over the $25,000, my father decided to sell the block of stores. And you'll never guess who was a member of the investment group buying the properties.

The dirty assessor.

Dad's attorney was Louis Karp, an experienced, savvy man who fought like hell for his clients and knew how to take advantage of an opportunity. My father had told Louis about paying the assessor, and the lawyer just nodded without comment.

The closing was scheduled for a Thursday, but the buyers called Louis and said they would have to delay until Friday. When Louis informed Dad, my father insisted that he wouldn't agree to the delay unless Louis got an extension in writing from the buyers.

Louis waved off my father's request. "Charlie, don't worry about it. Everything will be OK."

Friday came, and the lawyers, buyers, and my father were sitting around the table. The buyers' lawyer took out a sheet of paper with the purchase price and adjustments written on it and put it on the table. Louis stood up, moving his glasses down to the end of his nose, and scanned the numbers on the paper.

Then he said, "No, guys. That was the price yesterday. Today, the price is $25,000 more."

"What?" the buyers' lawyer asked.

Louis replied, "The price you wrote down was from yesterday. Now there's a new price."

Of course, this was why Louis didn't go along with my father's request that they get the extension in writing. The request for a delay enabled him to raise the price and recover Dad's payoff to the assessor. So the buyers paid the additional money, proving that sometimes people get what they deserve and that it never hurts to hire a smart lawyer.

# CHAPTER 7
# MY FIRST AUCTION

In 1963, my father bought 326 Dartmouth Street in Boston. It was a large, beautiful townhome on a wide corner lot and home to the German consulate.

Owning the property was uneventful. Then, in the early 1970s, my father had his eye on other properties and decided to sell to have more capital to invest. He sold the building to Dirk Patriarca from Rhode Island, an infamous surname in New England because it belonged to a crime family well-known to federal prosecutors, including Attorney General Robert F. Kennedy when he began pursuing organized crime.

Dirk (who passed away in 2014) wanted Dad to hold a second mortgage on the property, which he did, and from the beginning, it turned out to be a major headache.

By then, I was working with my father, and I remember being at his house in Belmont and hearing him making phone calls to delinquent tenants at night. He was also frequently talking to Dirk, who had fallen behind on his payments for the second mortgage.

"You're making me promises," my father would tell Dirk. "And you don't make the payments."

Dad was a cigar smoker, and Dirk kept promising to make him a humidor, an attempt to please him, but Dirk never came through with the humidor.

My father continued calling Dirk but after a while decided to foreclose. That meant he would get his money back by auctioning the property, and anything paid beyond the first and second mortgages would go to Dirk.

The day of the auction, my father and I were standing on the sidewalk outside the building with our attorney and the attorney for the bank that held the first mortgage. Dirk's handyman was also there with a group of spectators.

"What are you here for?" my father's attorney asked the handyman.

"I'm gonna bid on the property," he replied.

The attorney asked him, "Did you put up the deposit? Did you bring the check so you could bid?"

"Nah," he said.

"Then you can't bid," my father's attorney said.

The auctioneer opened up the bidding. The bank with the first mortgage put in a bid, and then my father's attorney put in a second bid that covered both mortgages. The auctioneer banged down his gavel, and the building was sold back to my father.

End of story, we thought.

Two minutes later, while we were doing the paperwork, Dirk flew down Dartmouth Street in his DeLorean, driving it onto the sidewalk and hopping out of the car.

"I'm here to bid," he announced.

"Too late," my father's attorney told him. "But we'll sell you the building. We don't want any profit. All we want is our original investment."

Dirk didn't want to hear of it. He was so angry that he ran up to the front of the building and smashed his fist into the plate glass in the French doors. The glass in those doors was heavy, a quarter-inch thick, and a piece fell down on the back of Dirk's wrist, cutting him. There was blood everywhere, and he had to go to the hospital.

Our offices were on the second floor of 176 Newbury Street. The broker and I were in the front office, the secretary was in the back, and my father was in a small side office by the secretary. Six months after Dirk got injured, he walked into Dad's office, shut the door, and pulled out a gun.

My father was at his desk and calmly said, "Dirk, I just want what I'm owed. Nothing else. You can have the property."

My father went through the legal means to transfer the property to him. Dirk used a straw buyer, a woman, who ended up taking title to the property, and my father got the money for the second mortgage.

That was the end of 326 Dartmouth Street. I have no idea why Dirk let it get to that point. I don't know if he didn't have the money or if he just didn't believe we would keep our word. The building was actually worth much more money, but we weren't interested in what wasn't ours.

I'd always thought real estate was an exciting game. However, this was a bit more excitement than I'd expected.

1952

(L to R) Me, Mom, Dad, and my sister in 1952.

My mother's parents, Nishan and Azniv Semonian, two of the wisest, kindest people I've ever met.

38 Whitten Street in Dorchester was a modest two-family house and the first building my parents owned.

OCT. 1956

69 Stony Brook Road, Belmont, Mass. (L to R) My sister Gail, me, my first cousin, M. Bruce Ohanian, and Dad. I would go with my father every weekend so he could check on the progress of the ranch house he was building. It didn't bother me at all not playing with my friends. I enjoyed watching the house going up piece by piece. I saw the foundation being poured, and when the wooden forms were removed, there were still the steel rods, side-by-side, going right through the cement, and these would also have to be taken out. This was the first job that Dad gave me.

232 Newbury Street, Back Bay, Boston. This was the beginning of my father's dream on Newbury. Back then, the street was just part of a sleepy neighborhood, and everyone thought if you rented, you rented to students My father had a different idea, and a year and a half after his death in 1987, the city of Boston honored his vision by adding a sign with the name, C. Talanian Way, at the intersection of Newbury and Exeter streets. By then, the company Dad had founded owned and managed seventeen buildings on the eight blocks of Newbury between Arlington Street and Massachusetts Avenue.

Washington Street. Braintree, Mass.
This was the first building Dad bought.
His father owned the stores next to it.

(L to R) My father, Neil Macintosh, and Charles Donovan, both of whom were brokers for Dad.

20

320 Commonwealth Avenue, in Back Bay, was the first building my father remodeled.

176 Newbury Street.

223 Beacon Street. My father bought this property in 1959. I sold it many years later.

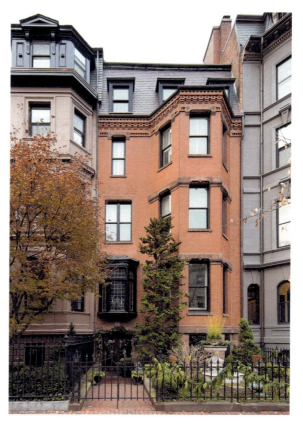

19 Marlborough Street, Back Bay, Boston. Not all of my father's plans panned out. In 1960, he bought 19 Marlborough, and ultimately 5, 7, 9, and 11, with an eye to knocking down those buildings. In retrospect, I can see that this was never going to happen. Because of their historical value, those buildings couldn't be torn down.

297 Newbury Street.

312 Marlborough Street. Our largest investment would become Newbury Street. However, Marlborough is where we discovered the advantages and disadvantages of owning a large swath of a street. After Dad passed away, I sold them because I wanted to shift into retail and commercial buildings. Yet I still miss Marlborough because these buildings are as beautiful as any residential properties in Boston. Evidently, John Singer Sargent, the artist born and bred in Boston, agreed with me He lived on the top floor of 312.

297 Newbury Street, after
our renovation.

125 -27 Fairview Avenue, Belmont.
125 Windsor Avenue, Watertown.
My mother's father, Nishan Simonian, bought these properties, and eventually gave me the place in Watertown, and my sister Gail the one in Belmont. Those gifts, in different ways, would have a profound impact on both of us.

303-305 Newbury Street.

My parents, Charles and Nevart Talanian.

303 305 Newbury Street, after our Renovation.jpg

312 Marlborough Street.

314 316 Newbury Street.

316 Newbury Street. We sold 314 and renovated 316.

# CHAPTER 8
# STREET OF DREAMS

———◆·◆·◆———

New York City has Fifth Avenue. Beverly Hills has Rodeo Drive. In Boston, we have Newbury Street, but I remember those beautiful brownstones and glittering shops when there was little beauty or glitter and it was possible, on any afternoon, to find a parking space.

Shortly after my father bought 232 Newbury, he purchased 176 Newbury. You entered the building by walking up seven stairs and going through a brownstone arch flanked by carved columns. Dom's Barbershop was in the basement, with the red-and-white barber pole out front. There was a shoe store on the first floor. C. Talanian Realty Company was on the second floor, and there were some other small offices people rented for their personal business. One woman rented space just to come in and do her paperwork and write checks.

Freestanding signs were allowed on the sidewalk in those days. We had a post outside to advertise C. Talanian Realty. There was also a corkboard out front where we pinned three-by-five cards listing properties for rent or things for sale. The shoe store also had several posts out front with a shoe lit up inside a large plastic ball. I was in high school at that time, and I remember the police were called to the building after a college student—I'm guessing he had a little alcohol in him—unscrewed one of the plastic shoe cases from the base, put it on his head so he resembled a Martian, and couldn't get it off. The story was written up in the paper.

My father bought 297 Newbury Street in 1964. Charlie Christopher probably opened the first organic food store in the Boston area in the basement, which also featured an asbestos-covered boiler. The store was called the Organic Food Cellar. I remember you could buy honey in bulk from a big, wooden barrel.

Upstairs, there were nine apartments that weren't in great condition. There was a tenant on the third floor. I don't recall his name, but he was the oldest vendor at Fenway Park. One day, I got a telephone call from a woman saying that mail was overflowing his mailbox. This was in 1970, not long after I'd started working for my father. He and my mother were in Florida for the winter so I went up to the apartment and rang the bell. No one answered. I knocked on the door. Again, no answer. In this case, our procedure was to use a master key, open the door a crack, and yell, "Hello? Anybody home?" I did that, heard nothing, and opened the door all the way. And there he was, the tenant, half on sofa and half on the floor, dead.

I felt terrible and called the police, who took him away.

His apartment was like something out of an old photograph. The kitchenette had yellowy enamel appliances with black, pin striping around the edge of the doors. The walls were as brown and gray as an old photograph. So now I had this place to fix up, and my father, before leaving for Florida, had gone to the bank and established a modest line of credit for me, maybe $2,000 at most, because the only thing we really spent money on in the winter was fuel oil.

My father watched every penny so I wanted to be cautious and got scared when upgrading the apartment approached $3,000. I had to strip the wallpaper, paint the walls, sand the floors, fix up the bathroom, and put in a new kitchenette with a new stove, refrigerator, sink, counter, and cabinets. That was my first big contracting job, and I rented it out for a decent price. That experience, particularly the importance of keeping your properties in good shape, was a lesson that has stayed with me throughout my career.

C. Talanian Realty continued acquiring buildings on Newbury Street. In 1977, we bought 215, and a year later, my dad made a decision that changed both our company and the retail landscape of Boston.

Massachusetts General Hospital had decided to sell three buildings that housed its Shepard-Gill School of Practical Nursing: 226, 228, and 230 Newbury Street. The broker who got those three properties for sale was smart. In those days, you went to the neighbor to see if they wanted to buy. That's an old-school move. If you have a property for sale, go to the neighbors on both sides and see if they're interested in buying it.

We already owned 232 Newbury Street, so when the broker approached Dad about the three properties, he was interested but also nervous because it was a big purchase for him in those days. The three buildings were part dormitory, part classroom, part cafeteria, and part storage. More like rooming houses. They didn't really have any character. We knew they were going to be sold vacant and needed total rehabs. My dad was doing some rough calculations on a paper napkin, but the truth is we guesstimated the overall cost based on our experience and the rental history of our other buildings.

Developers and property managers need to consider zoning before making a deal. Historically, Newbury Street was zoned for business only from Arlington to Exeter, and on that strip, there were always a lot of shops and no vacancies. The Massachusetts General properties were located between Exeter and Fairfield Street, and for three blocks, all the way over to Hereford Street, the zoning was residential. You'd see a store here and there, but mainly it was residential.

My father's view—and one I inherited—was that you have to keep your eyes on the horizon, not what's going on today around you. You plant seeds. You are patient. You wait.

We bought those three buildings, and combined with 232 Newbury, we were going to have eight stores and twenty-four apartments on Newbury. At that time, the Exeter Street Theater was still a theater. The Stephanie's Restaurant building was a parking lot, and next to it, in a small building, was the Massachusetts School of Optometry. The Nike building of today used to be a parking lot and the Prince School was a school.

Scuttlebutt among the real estate community was that my father was going to go broke because there was no business beyond Exeter Street. That all changed when zoning finally permitted commercial and residential west of Exeter. I calculated that if we dug out basements and created new stores for 226, 228, and 230, the rental income from those retail stores would come back to us in three years.

For architectural work, we hired the highly respected John Priestley. We took our plans to the Back Bay Architectural Commission. Initially, we weren't well received, but an architect on the board—I believe his name was John Johnson—took an interest.

"I think we've got something kind of special here," he told the board. He explained that the commission could make a statement of what they can do by partnering with a business that owned four buildings in a row to create "little jewel boxes of storefronts."

We still had to get the approval of the BBAC and the blessing of the Neighborhood Association of the Back Bay. They wanted to see blueprints and renderings, and we had to build a model. They acted as though we were aiming to put up another Prudential Center.

Dad was as nervous as I'd ever seen him due to the costs for the architectural plans and the model we were asked to build. Eventually, after much annoying back and forth with the BBAC and the neighborhood association, the project got approved. We renovated the buildings and had no problem renting them. Rent for the stores were $10 a square foot. Even with paying for architects, contractors, lawyers, the fees, and licenses, we earned back our investment in three years.

Those were the first major retail stores west of Exeter, and we continued collecting properties on Newbury. Actually, the legal address of the property at 303 Newbury was 52 Hereford Street because, according to the tax bill, the entrance was on Hereford. The basement had a bookstore and the office of Mr. Palmer, who used to be the city electrical inspector. He was working on his own as an electrician repairman, and I used his services for years. He was amazing. He'd wet his fingers, touch live circuits, and go, "Yep, that's a live one." I was glad he survived. In 1989, I renovated the building. The property became 303 and 305 Newbury because the first-floor store entrance was at 303 and 305. We converted six apartments into office space, which meant that we didn't have to put in six kitchens. This made the renovation cleaner, easier, and less expensive, and all the windows along the length of the building overlooked Newbury Street even though the entrance remained on Hereford.

At one point, C. Talanian Realty Company was the largest property owner on Newbury, and ultimately we were surpassed by two investment funds. I remember when my father was first buying properties on the street. Barry Hoffman, a member of the architectural commission and the Back Bay association, told the *Boston Business Journal*, "Charlie was a pioneer on Newbury Street."

Indeed he was. Dad passed away on July 27, 1987. He was seventy-one. I wish he'd had more time to enjoy his success and be with my mother, but I'm grateful that he lived long enough to see the beginning of his dream come true.

A year and a half after his death, my good friend of over twenty years, Joan Jolley, wrote to the city Boston requesting some type of recognition for my father's pioneering of retail space on Newbury. At that time, Joan was the head of the Newbury Street League. I was on the board, but I had no idea that she had written to the city. In the end, Boston honored my father by adding a sign with the name C. Talanian Way at the intersection of Newbury and Exeter streets. By then, the company Dad had founded owned and managed seventeen buildings on the eight blocks of Newbury between Arlington Street and Massachusetts Avenue.

At the ceremony, I learned something else about my dad that made me incredibly proud. As the photographers were taking pictures, my sister and I noticed a Black fellow standing off to the side. Gail asked him why he was attending the ceremony, and he told us that he had come to honor our father because years ago when he had come to Boston for law school, Mr. Talanian was the only landlord he spoke to who would rent him an apartment.

I didn't find that story the least bit strange. My father was a one-on-one man. He believed in people and sized you up, and his perception determined how he treated you. Race, religion, or where you born played no part in his judgment.

Dad wouldn't have been surprised by the blossoming of Newbury Street into the premier shopping street in Boston. For the first four buildings he bought and renovated, he paid approximately half a million dollars. In fact, when he died, his total portfolio, exclusive of mortgages, may have been worth $11 million. Today, by my guess, just the combined value of those properties is $60 million.

And that, I am sure, he would not believe.

# CHAPTER 9
# A DEAL'S A DEAL

One morning in 1970, after driving into Boston from his home, my father was sitting in his car and waiting at the red light on the corner of Gloucester and Boylston streets. He noticed a real estate broker we referred to as Old Man Epps. He was an old Bostonian whose jacket pockets were always stuffed with his listings. The man was a walking office. He also wore two pairs of glasses, or maybe even three, all the time so he could see. In short, he was a genuine character. When my father saw Old Man Epps coming out of the building, he rolled down his window and called out, "Is it for sale?"

"Yeah," Epps said. "For fifty thousand."

Dad replied, "How about forty-eight?"

"Deal!" Epps shouted.

I'm sure Dad checked whether the building was a worthwhile investment, and he did learn that it needed a total renovation, so saving that $2,000 was helpful. In those days, when properties in that part of Boston sold for $20,000 or $30,000, and occasionally as high as $100,000, saving a couple of thousand dollars was no small thing. Today, with the properties selling in the millions, we do a lot more due diligence before making an offer, but I treasure this story of Dad and Epps cutting a deal at a red light.

I worked on the building with the contractor and the laborers, painting the hallways and doing some carpentry. I always have a toolbox in the trunk of my car and at home, where I continue to do repairs myself and 80 percent of the maintenance. The 20 percent of the stuff I can't fix, I can usually diagnose the problem and pass along the information to whomever has come to do the work. I must say that I have a habit of going over the contractors' bills to make sure I'm not overpaying for materials and time charges.

When we were done with 51 Gloucester and finished leasing it, we had a small one-bedroom apartment in the basement, a retail store on the first floor, two small, one-bedrooms on the second floor, and a three-bedroom on the top floor.

A retired saxophonist lived in the basement apartment, and he loved to talk and could keep you busy for an hour if you happened to run into him. He stopped paying rent, and my father phoned him on a regular basis, offering to help him come up with a payment plan. The saxophonist had a host of creative excuses for why he wasn't paying, and Dad finally got him to agree to come down our office and pay his rent. When the saxophonist arrived, however, he claimed that he was bringing in the money but got robbed on Newbury Street. Eventually, we had to evict him and take our loss.

The top floor we rented to a guy who had a regular gig playing the piano at a gay bar in Bay Village, Boston's smallest official neighborhood. He paid his deposit and moved in but never paid rent. In a way, this stuff was not atypical back then. We didn't do exhaustive background checks on tenants beyond their salary and a recommendation, if available, from a previous landlord.

I was angry at the piano player for giving us such a hard time, because I knew he was earning enough to pay. I decided to avoid the hassle and expense of legally evicting him. Instead, I contacted a friend of mine in Waltham. He had a dark complexion and a very round face, and he resembled a hit man. The fact that he drove a Lincoln Continental with red, crushed, velvet upholstery was a bonus. Then I called my cousin, a big guy who also bore a faint resemblance to a contract killer, and another friend,

Chuckie, tall and lanky with a cigarette hanging out of his mouth. The four of us went to the bar, gave the doorman $20, and asked him to watch the car.

Inside, I sat at a table with my back to the piano with my three accomplices sitting across from me. I told the waitress that after the piano guy finished his set, we'd like to speak to him.

He came over to the table, smiling, until he spotted me, and his smile vanished.

"Have a seat," I said.

He sat down, and the other guys went into their routine, saying, "We understand you're not paying Mr. Talanian. It's really not right. You moved into a brand-new apartment. You gave a deposit. You signed the lease and you pay nothing, and it's been four months. You know you can't play a piano if you have broken fingers."

Then we stood up and walked out. The next morning, he came to the office and paid all the rent he owed. And he was never late again.

Not exactly a legal solution to my problem, but a satisfying one.

Ultimately, the piano player moved, and I had three dental hygienists live in the apartment. They were meticulous about paying their rent. One day, one of them called me and said, "Charles, we have a mouse problem. Can you send someone up or take care of it?"

I handled it by putting some glue boards down around the baseboards and radiators, and I didn't hear about the mice again.

A few months later, a hygienist called to request a small repair, and I asked, "Did the mouse problem get taken care of? You never called back."

"Not really," she said. "We just cut off the legs and throw the mice down the toilet and leave the glue board alone."

I went up to their apartment, and there must have been a hundred feet stuck on those glue boards. Those women had a lot of guts. I put down new boards and sent in a professional exterminator.

I've had some tenants, residential and commercial, for over thirty years. They are always on time with the rent and communicate when they can't pay. It's great that they have the courage to call and keep me in the loop if they are going through a hard time. Then I'll say, "Take a week, take ten days if you need it, as long as you're being upfront with me. That's all I care about."

The truth is that tenants need landlords and landlords need tenants, and the overwhelming majority of people keep their word. Of course, as the neighborhood had become so much more expensive, the tenants are in a different economic league than in the old days. Now we do a thorough check on the financial health of possible tenants, especially large commercial clients. We look into their financial history. Sometimes, we initially take six months' rent as part of their deal, or even a year's letter of credit. That happens when the tenant wants to sign a corporate signature to protect himself in the event of bankruptcy. If you have the letter of credit, you can't get stuck because if they fail to pay you, just take the letter to the bank it's drawn on and get paid.

The recommendation from previous, and reliable, landlords is helpful. There seems to be an unwritten code that a landlord won't give another landlord a bad tenant. I've been told not to rent to some prospective tenant because they don't pay.

When I started out, there was a lot of honor in the real estate community. One building owner's son, Marty Berman, was an insurance person who taught courses at Bentley University in Waltham. He used to tell the story of his father selling two or three buildings in a package to Charlie Talanian on a handshake and how people would offer him more money before the agreements were drawn up and signed, but he'd say, "No, I shook hands, and a deal's a deal."

I must confess that in those days, it was more fun being in the real estate business.

# CHAPTER 10
# THE GIFT

My maternal grandparents, Azniv and Nishan Simonian, were born in Harput, Armenia. Many people are familiar with the Armenian Genocide, but there was earlier mass violence in 1894, the Hamidian massacres, the name derived from the sultan who incited it, Abdul Hamid II. Casualties were estimated in the hundreds of thousands, and fortunately my grandparents escaped, arriving at Ellis Island in 1896.

I don't know much about their parents or their childhoods, but I do know that my grandmother was six or seven years old when she arrived in the United States. She had two sisters (and later a brother who was born in America and became a doctor in Providence, Rhode Island). I remember Grammy telling me that as she stood in line at Ellis Island an official marked her coat with an X. She didn't say anything else about it for years, and I was in my fifties when I learned the rest of the story. There were doctors at Ellis Island who looked you over, and if they thought you had an ailment they would mark you, which meant you were going to be sent back—in my grandmother's case, probably to die in a massacre. Frightened, Grammy stood there, and the woman behind her said, "Your coat is very good quality and has a good lining. If you turn it inside out, they won't know."

So my grandmother turned her coat inside out and got through Ellis Island.

My lasting impression of my grandparents is that they were so grateful for their American life. They appreciated the opportunity the country gave them to prosper and all of the conveniences that appeared during their lives—from refrigerators to jet airplanes. Their marriage had been arranged, but my grandfather wasn't a stickler for the old country traditions. For instance, he wanted Grammy to get a driver's license, which was far from typical back then when men were supposed to do all the driving. I'm happy he did because Grammy took Gail and me to the movies, beaches, zoos, and amusement parks. She loved us, and her love was obvious even to a child.

Dede, my grandfather, was as generous a man as I've ever known. His generosity, I believe, was rooted in the deprivations of his childhood. He was also a man of his word. Thus, in 1966, when a priest asked to him to buy two houses for the church and then changed his mind, my grandfather felt that because he had already made a deal with the sellers, he couldn't back out and bought the two-family houses anyway, one at 129 Windsor Avenue in Watertown and the other at 125–127 Fairview Avenue in Belmont. He gave me the place in Watertown, and my sister Gail the one in Belmont. Those gifts, in different ways, would have a profound impact on both of us.

I was twenty when I received Dede's gift. The first-floor unit was rented for $50 a month, and the second floor for $75. The house was old and needed new kitchens, bathrooms, and boilers, and it still had fuses instead of circuit breakers. I didn't use the money for myself but plowed every nickel back into the house. I learned that lesson from watching my father, who increased the value of his portfolio by hiring contractors and doing some of the work himself. I enjoyed the process and the results of creating wealth via elbow grease.

Once the house was in better shape, I thought it was only fair that my renter paying $50 a month should pay $75, and he agreed. The problem was he never paid the additional money. I kept telling him that he owed me $25 more every month, but he refused to pay. He had a wife and two children, and I felt terrible when it became clear he had no intention of paying. I had to evict him. I hired Bobby Mardirosian, a well-known Armenian attorney in Watertown, and got my first taste of how legally difficult it is to get a renter who isn't paying the rent to leave. And expensive. When it was over, I owed Bobby $4,000, and I had no idea where I was going to find that amount of money. Over time, I managed to scrape it together, but the whole process was the most unpleasant business experience I'd had up to that point.

I owned that building for eight or nine years, and it shaped my entire philosophy of managing real estate—that keeping a building in excellent shape, though a financial drain in the short run, will eventually pay off. By the time I sold it for $110,000, I was getting $800 a floor in rent. A broker called me and asked, "Did you really sell that property for $110,000? That's ten thousand more than these two-family houses usually sell for."

I could have held onto the house for another decade, but then I would have to redo it again. I sold it because I figured I had maxed out my return, and I would repeat this buy-and-sell philosophy after determining that you could you apply the approach to a $100,000 building or one valued at $10 million. I used the money from selling Windsor to purchase 1695–1697 Commonwealth Avenue in Alston, and that building would become the paradigm for my entire career.

# CHAPTER 11
# GOVERNMENT MYOPIA

My father was a fan of assumable mortgages. In a thirty-year mortgage, 99 percent of the monthly bill is interest, and the rest is principal. So in 1978 when Dad found 1043 and 1045 Beacon Street in Brookline, side-by-side brick, bow-front buildings, had assumable mortgages, he bought them from a widow who was taking care of the buildings with some help from her daughter. She had already paid off much of the interest during the first fifteen years and was reducing the principal, which meant that my father could own the buildings free and clear in a compressed amount of time.

The buildings were under rent control. Residents were paying $16 to $22 a week for a room. I remember one Thanksgiving morning, I got a call that someone on the top floor had toppled over the railing, fell four stories to the floor, and died. We had to call the police to get over there and figure out what happened. Evidently, the deceased had been drinking the night before. The police inspected the scene, but there had been nothing wrong with the building, and the banister hadn't broken.

Inspectors arrived twice a year from the building, fire, and egress departments, and they would send us a list of things that needed fixing—a broken switch plate or peeling linoleum, minor cosmetic things. I had put together a set of plans because the buildings had no parking, so I created parking in the rear by filling in a lower courtyard in back.

My father and I planned to turn the buildings into two- and three-bedroom condominiums to make them family oriented rather than small units for single people. Our plan was rejected by the Town of Brookline because the buildings were under rent control. As residents left, I didn't rerent the units. I locked them up and decided to keep them empty to see how quickly the buildings would vacate and then try for a condominium conversion again.

A student who lived in one of the units, a guy in his late twenties or early thirties, was a strange character who dressed in a trench coat with the collar up and walked down the street as if he were a detective. After eighteen months, only four units were still occupied. This trench coat person realized that I was not rerenting the units and complained to the rent-control board. Brookline brought a suit against me, and the inspectors moved in right away to reinspect the buildings. I ended up with pages of things that were wrong after years and years of getting half-page reports of minor things. Now it was like I had to remodel the place.

I hired an attorney to fight the charges, but I was found guilty for not rerenting apartments, which was my obligation to do under rent-control laws. I was a white-collar criminal. I was told that I couldn't leave the country without permission.

Shortly after the court ruled, I had to travel overseas, and I was able to get permission to go. When I returned, I started thinking about what had happened in court. It certainly wasn't sitting well with me that I was taking care of the property and paying the upkeep and taxes, all while the Town of Brookline was telling me what I could charge for a unit. And I asked myself, "Do you work for Brookline?"

"No," I answered. "I do not."

The word *license* rings a bell in my head. It's a privilege. Not everyone has one. I did, though—a rooming house license. What if I didn't want it?

I picked up the phone and called various organizations to ask if they would like to triple-net lease a building for a dollar a year. That way, Brookline wouldn't be annoying me, and I'd own the buildings until I had the opportunity to convert them to condos.

At the time, Kitty Dukakis, the governor's wife, was close to the monsignor of Boston. They were working with the Pine Street Inn, which became interested in the two buildings. The Pine Street Inn, near the expressway, provided meals and shelter for the homeless. The group was looking for a halfway house, and they didn't want to lease from me; they wanted to buy the two buildings. So I put a fair price tag on them, and they agreed to buy. Now we had to go for a hearing because I was also selling the rooming house license. The meeting was standing room only, and most of the audience was more than a little annoyed. There were people holding up signs with pictures of the homeless sleeping on the sidewalk or with the words "I'D RATHER HAVE CONDOS" printed in big, bold letters. Kitty Dukakis and the monsignor attended the hearing with their attorney, and I was able to sell to them. I was happy to walk away. I couldn't stand the experience and just wanted to put it behind me.

But there is a lesson here for communities practicing rent control. Had Brookline not forced that on me, I would've converted the buildings, and the bottom line is Brookline would've collected much more in tax revenue from the new owners than they would've collected from me. And if Brookline wanted to help the homeless—a noble cause—the town could have issued credit vouchers for the unfortunate to rent places to live. In fact, there was a motel directly across the street from the rooming houses.

Tragically, government is rarely that smart. Instead, they destroy property values and decrease the public coffers, which helps no one.

# CHAPTER 12
# THE PARADIGM

There were two brick buildings, side by side, and they sat high on a hill in Brighton, out by Cleveland Circle and Boston College.

The owner was Abraham Kellem of Hull, Massachusetts, my father's plumber. This was back in the 1970s when plumbers could afford to own a pair of buildings in Brighton. And Abe Kellem was a real professional. He had an office in the South End on Tremont Street. He used to wear blue jean shirts with the top button buttoned, and he always had rubbers on his shoes. When he went into someone's house, he removed the rubbers so his shoes wouldn't soil the carpet. Instead of trucks, Abe worked out of a hearse because that was the only vehicle long enough for twelve-foot pipes.

Abe decided he wanted to sell the buildings, and one day he asked me if I was interested in buying them. I had never bought a building on my own before; I was managing my father's properties for less than a hundred dollars a week and was eager to own property. I knew I could turn a profit on the two-family in Watertown that my grandfather had given to me and figured I could use that money to buy a substantial rental property.

I looked over Abe's properties. He obviously hadn't spent much updating them. If I remember correctly, there were harvest-gold stoves and avocado-green refrigerators. But Abe had taken good care of the plumbing so I wouldn't have to waste money replacing pipes. There were thirteen rental units, five of them rent controlled, but the noncontrolled rents were below the going market rate, and the buildings were perfect fixer-uppers in need of new kitchens, bathrooms, and a cosmetic makeover. This work wouldn't be too expensive, especially because I could do some of it myself.

I don't recall what I paid for the buildings, but I thought it was a good price. And with a down payment from selling my two-family house, I got a first mortgage, and Abe gave me a second mortgage.

My father didn't interfere, but he owned ten properties by then, and I let him know what I was doing. He would nod his head and agree and maybe give me a suggestion or two. I was smart enough to listen to him, and in retrospect I can see that my approach closely followed how he had built his portfolio.

Every nickel I made in rent, I put back into the buildings. I started with the public areas. I installed new mailboxes by the front doors, and I painted the hallways, put down carpeting, and put up new light fixtures. When I finished, I raised the rent of the noncontrolled apartments to market rate. Some tenants stayed, others left, which was fine because it gave me the opportunity to go into their units and repaint and put in modern kitchens and modern baths, paint the place, and make the apartment look as new as the public areas.

Once an apartment was renovated, I'd take a potential renter in to show it, he'd see the upgrades, and I could charge a decent rent. I continued doing that with all the apartments; I owned the building for six or seven years. During that time, many people vacated, allowing me to redo their apartments, and when I finally sold, there was only one rent-controlled apartment.

I walked away with $400,000 in profit. I felt as though I had arrived, and that money enabled me to buy far more expensive properties. But the most valuable result of my owning the buildings in Brighton was that I established a paradigm for how to be a big-time landlord, using the rents to improve your properties and creating your own value month by month until you had reached a maximum value, then selling and trading up to bigger and better properties with a higher return.

My father had done this. And now I was doing it for myself.

# CHAPTER 13
# JANE

You never think that one afternoon, sitting in your office looking through paperwork, your life will be changed forever, but that happened to me in 1980 when Jane Chapman stopped by to check if we had any listings she could pitch to her clients. Jane was a dark-haired beauty, twenty-six years old, and a broker at Cabot & Company, a real estate firm not far from us on Newbury Street.

I was happy showing her our listings because it gave me a chance to think up other things to say and keep Jane sitting across from me. As often happens with people in Boston, our conversation drifted to the cape. I owned a lot in the New Seabury Resort and Country Club in Mashpee. I hadn't built a place yet, but by owning that property, I was permitted to join the beach and golf club and often went down in the summer to play. As luck would have it, Jane's parents had a home in New Seabury, and she frequently visited them, so I asked for her parents' phone number and said I'd call when I came to the cape.

Never one to let an opportunity to pass by, I called the following week. Her mother answered, and I said, "Hello, Mrs. Chapman. This is Charles Talanian. Is Jane in?"

Her mother hesitated. Then she told me to hold on, and Jane came on the phone. I asked her to dinner, and she agreed. I picked up Jane and met her parents, Rita and Raymond, her aunt Peg, and her sister Judy.

We ate at Chillingsworth, a fancy restaurant in Brewster, and I'll never forget the first comment Jane made. "My mother said I better tell you my maiden name. It's Abdella. We're Lebanese."

Frankly, I felt so wonderful in Jane's company that I wouldn't have cared if her family were from Mars. Jane had picked up the last name of Chapman from her ex-husband, Peter Chapman, who played the lead trumpet in the Boston Symphony Orchestra.

We talked for hours over dinner, and the next week, in Boston, we met for lunch at the Harvard Bookstore Café. Jane had some additional information for me. For the last four years, she had been receiving treatment for maxillofacial cylindroma, a cancer so rare that Jane would appear at a medical convention to discuss her case with four hundred doctors. There was a dot at the corner of her eye where the radiation was directed. Her oncologist and Jane were optimistic. I was in love, which creates its own faith in the future. And because I was certain that Jane would recover, I saw no reason for us not to be involved.

Originally, our parents objected to our relationship in a way that brought to mind the Hatfields and McCoys. Rita and Raymond, I believe, wanted Jane to marry someone who was Lebanese or who was closer to that than I was. My parents hoped I'd find an Armenian girl, and preferably one who wasn't being treated for cancer.

To avoid any familial unpleasantness, Jane and I eloped on Friday, December 3, 1982, marrying before a judge at the courthouse in Cambridge. We lived in my two-bedroom condo in a high-rise at 131 Coolidge Avenue in Watertown, right on the Charles River overlooking the Boston skyline. I had bought a preconstruction unit there in 1975. It was being built by the same gentleman who had built 10 Williams Street, where I'd lived before and which I'd been fortunate enough to sell for twice what I paid for it. Watertown was very affordable, and I had easy access to Boston driving down the Back River Road and onto Storrow Drive.

These were wonderful years for Jane and me, even though she was still battling cancer. We went to New York City for a consultation with an oncologist at Memorial Sloan Kettering. He said, "I'm not going to be as nice to you as the doctors in Boston. I suggest removing your nose and replacing it with a prosthetic."

Jane and I looked at each other. Clearly, that wasn't an option she was ready to consider, especially as we walked out of his office and saw one of his patients coming in with a gauze triangle on her face where her nose had been.

Jane began researching alternative treatments. We were in California, Mexico, and Canada talking to doctors. Jane subscribed to a $10 flyer on Cape Cod in which people would publish things about medications that had worked or hadn't worked for them, and in this flyer, she kept seeing a doctor's name, Hans Nieper, who practiced in Hannover, West Germany.

At about this time, Jane sold a condominium on Beacon Street to a couple from California and Colorado. The couple also bought a beach bungalow in New Seabury up on a bluff overlooking the ocean, and they wanted to have dinner with us in Mashpee. We went to the Flume, a restaurant with excellent food. The woman was very Hollywood—she used to write for *The Mary Tyler Moore Show*—and Jane asked her if she'd ever heard anyone mention a Dr. Hans Nieper.

"Actually, yes," the woman replied. "The actor Fred MacMurray from the TV series *My Three Sons*, his wife was diagnosed with throat cancer and told that she had six months to live, and they ended up going to see Dr. Nieper."

"How long ago was her diagnosis?" Jane asked.

Six years was the answer, and the woman gave Jane MacMurray's telephone number. We called him in California, and he gave us all the information we needed. We were scheduled to see a doctor in Switzerland, so after talking to him, we arranged to speak with Dr. Nieper in West Germany.

He was a brilliant man who focused on strengthening the immune system and believed a beefed-up immune system would fight the cancer. He prescribed natural pills, oils, and powders, and the routine for taking them. He would do blood work, send it to his laboratory in Switzerland, and—based on the feedback—alter the routine a little bit every six months. We spent two weeks in Hannover, and Jane saw him every day. We returned for annual appointments.

At home, Jane would have her blood work done through her sister Judy, who was the head of special chemistry at a local hospital. After seeing Dr. Nieper annually for three years, he said, "Here's a tube. Send me a blood sample in six months, and I can alter your routine."

Jane brought the tube back to Judy who said, "You can't send blood in a tube."

Well, in that tube you could. It had special chemicals to preserve the blood. So now, every six months, Jane was receiving an update on her status and told what to take and what not to take. It was all pills, powders, drinks, carrot juice, and sometimes injections that I would give her.

This went on for the next fourteen years.

# CHAPTER 14
# OUR MIRACLE CHILD

———◆•◆•◆———

We weren't sure that Jane could have children, and then, lo and behold, in 1984, she became pregnant and made it into the second trimester without any complications.

Jane was very brave facing cancer, and because of her bravery, and Dr. Nieper keeping the illness at bay, our optimism held. We began looking to move to a more spacious home.

I wanted to be within walking distance to the office, and we found a lovely townhouse, built in 1910, with a granite and brick façade, a grand entry foyer, and gorgeous woodwork. It was a corner building with three entrances and had been built by a Dr. Bradbury, and I believe it was the first building in the United States where more than one dentist practiced together. The residential entrance was at 16 Exeter Street; the commercial entrances were at 196 and 198 Marlborough Street.

The building needed updating to make it ready for us, and I moved into the top floor unit—basically, with a mattress on the floor—to oversee the work while Jane, two weeks from her planned C-section, went to live at her parents' condo in Needham. (We had already sold our place in Watertown.) The only phone available at the Exeter house was the construction phone on the second floor. One night, I woke up and heard it ringing. I was half-asleep, reluctant to get out from under the covers to answer it, and made a deal with myself that I'd only go down if it rang one more time. Sure enough, it rang again, and I took off down the stairs. Good thing I did because Jane was on the line saying that she was on her way to Brigham and Women's Hospital and I should meet her there.

Our son Christopher was born on October 3, 1985. He was our miracle, and my parents' only grandchild. My father's birthday was on October 4, and that year, my mother had planned a seventieth birthday party for him at Winchester Country Club. The party was held on the third so we were at the hospital and missed it, but I called Dad, and he was so excited he ran out to a cigar store and passed out cigars at the country club.

Shortly after Chris arrived, we moved into our new home. I had converted the apartments on the second and third floors to a duplex for living, retained the three-bedroom apartment for us on the top floor, and kept the basement and first floor for income purposes.

As we unpacked, the work was ongoing—light bulb sockets were hanging out of the electrical boxes on the walls, which were still only primed. My father used to stop by in the mornings and come upstairs while I was feeding Chris. He'd look around and say, "You should paint it Florida style—white."

The estimate I'd received to paint the townhouse was $30,000, and I'd reply, "Dad, if I could afford the painting, I'd pick a color."

Slowly but surely the work was completed. Jane and I wanted to have another child. However, she was having trouble getting pregnant. Jane thought we should adopt a girl from Lebanon. That was fine with me, and we were told by the adoption agency that we'd have a better chance at adopting if we had a church wedding. So in 1988, at the Armenian Holy Trinity Church on Brattle Street in Cambridge, Jane and I were married by a priest with three-year-old Christopher and a couple with whom we were close as witnesses.

We never did adopt a Lebanese child. There were too many stories of children from drug-addicted mothers and with other serious health issues, and we decided that we should count our blessings for having a healthy son. Jane was an attentive mother, overly attentive in my view, and our relationship was altered by her focus on Christopher. I suppose this feeling isn't uncommon among fathers after a first child is born. According to Jane, her mother had pushed her father aside and focused mainly on their daughters. Still, her mother dished out a fair number of responsibilities to her daughters, while Jane didn't take this tact with our son even as Chris got older. Many times I told Jane, "You weren't brought up this way. You had a job in high school during the summer months. Your mother and father both worked most of their lives. You had to come home from school and start the dinner. You had responsibilities, and I did too. I'd cut grass for five dollars if I could in the summertime, and I worked all sorts of jobs."

I never changed her mind or her approach. Now given what would happen, I've wondered whether Jane, sensing that, due to her cancer, her time with Christopher would be cut short, and she wanted to fill him up with as much love as possible so he could withstand the coming loss and know, that although he didn't have his mother for long, that she loved him enough to last Chris a lifetime.

I decided that the best way to deal with Jane's cancer was to believe in the future, and I started planning to build a house on Cape Cod. The house had been a dream of mine for years. Twice a month, after work, I'd take the subway to talk to an architect in Harvard Square. Jane commented that if I didn't bring a home a set of plans, she'd think I'd joined a secret organization.

I first became involved with real estate on the cape in 1970 when I bought a buildable lot in Fells Pond in New Seabury for $4,000. As a recent college graduate, I didn't have the money to build, but owning the land gave me access to the beach and country club. My aunt lived in that same neighborhood, and so did Jane's parents. We used to visit them on weekends, and I realized that I was going to be on the cape. I didn't want to be in the woods, which was where my lot was located. I preferred to be on a marsh or the water, a spot that had view of the horizon.

In the mornings on those weekends, I'd drive from New Seabury to Great Neck Road South and down to the Dick and Ellie's Flea Market, where I had coffee and chatted with Dick and Ellie, two lovely people. Later, I'd drive by waterfront homes. I saw a beauty on Popponesset Island with its own dock, but the price was a quarter of million dollars, which I couldn't afford. I was talking to a broker and mentioned that as I approached the Mashpee Rotary, I noticed water on my right.

"That's Popponesset Bay and Ockway Bay," she said. "There's a ten-acre parcel that's coming up for sale. There's a lot of interest in it. The owners are going to accept closed bids."

In 1979, I hadn't planned on being a developer on the cape. All I wanted was an escape from Boston in the summer. The problem was that I couldn't afford to buy a house with a view. So I found a partner to bid with me, and we won, paying $117,000 for ten acres on the water. We put in the road, utilities, gas, water, and telephone and sold off the lots. In the end, he kept one for himself and I took the lot on the point.

Still, I'm a conservative investor, and I like to keep my debt in line with my holdings. And I didn't have the resources to build. On the other hand, I had a bubbly toddler and a sick wife with an uncertain future. I had a talk with myself about what truly matters in life, and then I went to Brookline Savings Bank and borrowed half a million dollars after planning the house for seven years. I built the house at 29 Ockway Bay Road in Mashpee, landscaped the grounds, bought a Jeep and a small boat, and we moved in before the summer of 1989.

*Finally,* I thought, *you have everything a man could want.*

What I didn't think was that nothing lasts forever.

# CHAPTER 15
# MATH-AND-
# SCIENCE WING

In 1995 and 1996, Jane's cancer spread. She had no choice other than surgery, and three surgeons operated on her for thirty-three hours. Half of her face was removed—her eye, her cheekbone, her upper palate, and her nose. She remained in the hospital for a month. The surgeons performed skin grafts and pieced Jane back together. They took a bone from inside her leg and put cuts in it so they could bend it to create a jawbone. They put in posts for teeth. They had to make an upper lip with other parts of her body. Through it all, Jane was unimaginably brave. Because she hated leaving Christopher and me, she went through procedures in doctors' offices instead of checking into a hospital for days.

Once Jane got up and going again, it would bother her when we walked down the street. She would get herself dressed up and put together as best she could, but children would stare at her, and she would get upset that parents wouldn't discipline the children by saying, "Don't stare at the lady." Yet when I saw adults look at her, I could see the fear in their faces. They couldn't comprehend what they were looking at. Jane had been an absolutely beautiful woman—a heart-shaped face with lovely features, almond eyes, and dark skin. Now that was gone.

And all I could do was thank God she was alive.

Meanwhile, we had a son to raise. The rush was on to find Chris a private school. Admissions were competitive, and it was nerve-racking attending the open houses and making certain the applications were in on time. Chris enrolled at Dexter Southfield School in Brookline. The bus would pick him up in Back Bay, and he had to wear a cap and blazer. In first and second grades, they taught the children public speaking in front of hundreds of people. It was funny. Even though the microphone was down as low as it could go, some of the children had to stand on their toes to reach it. Dexter was a great experience for Chris, but it didn't have a high school as it does today so we had to make other arrangements, which unfortunately created a conflict between Jane and me. I hated arguing with her, especially now that she was so sick, but I thought I was doing what was best for our son.

Boarding school had helped turn my life around, and I knew it would be good for Chris. Jane didn't want her little boy going away. She wanted Chris to go to a Catholic school, St. Sebastian's in Needham. It was a smaller school than Dexter and right across the street from where her parents lived. It drove me crazy. I knew he wouldn't be happy there. I have nothing against religion, but it is a Catholic school with religion a part of the student's regular classroom learning. And I didn't want Chris at his grandparents' every day. I wanted him to be independent, to start the psychological transition to adulthood. And though I couldn't say it, Chris was going to be growing up faster than most. I doubted that his mother would be alive for his college graduation.

Reluctantly, Jane accompanied Chris and me to the open house at Tabor Academy, a boarding school with an excellent reputation and a large, beautiful campus in Marion, Massachusetts, a small town fifty-nine miles south of Boston and situated on Sippican Harbor. The students looked sharp in their blazers. In some of the other schools we visited, the students were in sweatshirts, baggy pants, and had hair dyed royal-blue or lime-green, all of them just slouching around.

Following the tour, we had lunch on the campus and happened to be seated beside the Tabor headmaster, Jay Stroud. Jane gave him the third degree, and Jay patiently answered every one of her questions. No way she could argue with the guy. He was fabulous. And I caught a break because Chris really liked Tabor and announced that he wanted to go there, so I didn't have to debate with Jane. It worked out well for Chris. He got a first-rate education and made lifelong friends.

I was impressed with Jay Stroud—his sense of educational mission and his intelligence. We used to meet for lunch when he was down my way, and Jane and I decided to donate $500,000 to Tabor to support the renovation of a math-and-science wing.

Jay was grateful and said that usually people waited to see what Tabor could do for their children before donating. That wasn't Jane and me. If Chris was going to school there, we were happy to help. I was also glad to be in a financial position to give away that kind of money. But during one of my lunches with Jay, I discovered a meaning to my career that I'd never seen so clearly before.

Looking out the window to a building that was going up, I said, "I'm putting up that place across the street. There are two hundred guys on the site, and I can't believe I'm the one paying them."

Yet that realization was more than a measure of my success. It was what my success meant to the people I employed—a way to support their families and to help carve out a future for their children. I was proud of that, as proud as I've been of anything I'd ever accomplished.

# CHAPTER 16
# ESCAPE: THE BAHAMAS

———— ◆·◆·◆ ————

I prided myself on being a one-step-at-a-time real estate investor, building a portfolio over decades by buying and maintaining decent buildings in desirable locations. I've never chased the quick buck or huge returns. I was my father's student, and he taught me that the deadliest enemy in the real estate game was impatience and greed.

All I can say about the small fortune I lost in the Bahamas is that it wasn't the most clear-thinking time in my life. Jane was dying in slow motion.

The roots of my Bahamian miscalculation were in the late 1990s. Jane, Chris, and I used to visit my mother in Boca Raton, Florida, and stay at the Boca Hotel and Beach Resort, which had a pleasant lounge where you could meet people and socialize and put together a golf foursome. It was nice staying there. I knew Jane didn't want to move to Florida, and she didn't want me commuting from Boston to be in Florida on the weekends. And finally, as much as I enjoyed Florida, the weather in January and February could be too chilly.

One day, I was leafing through one of my mother's magazines and spotted a small block ad about a Bahamas hotel with a Greg Norman-designed golf course and deep-water marina. Usually you can't put both of those together: you can have a hell of a golf course or a hotel on the ocean. I was intrigued, called the number in the ad, and spoke to a realtor in Delray Beach. His last name was De Niro, and he claimed to be related to the famous actor. I made arrangements to fly with him on a private, twin-engine plane to Great Exuma, Bahamas, to scout the property.

The project would be named Emerald Bay, but the site was a horror show. There was a cinderblock building with no windows or roof, and from what I could tell, there was no construction going on—not even footprints or tire tracks in the sand. Disappointed, I flew home.

A while later, I received call from Kevin Clemente, the executive director of the project. As a student at Boston College, Kevin had been cocaptain of the football team and now lived in Albany, New York, where I had owned property. We became friends. Kevin explained that construction had stopped until they could find a hotel with which to partner so the residents of Emerald Bay would have the amenities expected at a resort.

Kevin and I talked occasionally, and one afternoon he told me that he was close to a deal with the luxurious Four Seasons Hotel.

Shortly after I spoke to Kevin, I was invited to dinner at the White House with forty successful Armenians. It was during the Clinton administration, and I was asked because of the hotel we were renovating in Armenia. Levon Ter-Petrosyan, the president of Armenia was there, and I spoke to Vice President Al Gore, but it was my conversation with a friend, Carl Bazarian, that decided me on the Bahamas. Carl was a Third World, emerging-markets hotel broker, and he had put the Marriott deal together in Armenia.

I asked Carl if he had heard anything about the Four Seasons going to Exuma, and he looked stunned. "I did that deal," he replied. "It's all done. It was signed last Friday. How'd you know about that?"

"Because I've been looking at that island for two years."

That week, I called Kevin Clemente and became the first person to buy a lot, paying $525,000, which was quite pricey for the Bahamas. I thought it was a smart move, figuring that there was a Four Seasons Hotel plus a casino, a Greg Norman golf course, and a deep-water marina. It doesn't get any better than that.

I designed the house with a wonderful architect in Boca Raton and hired a builder, and once a month, I'd go to the Bahamas, check into the Four Seasons by myself, play a little golf, and watch the house going up. I knew it was a distraction from my sadness about Jane and the helplessness that sets in when you can't save a loved one.

Our last Christmas together as a family was in 2003. Jane did not feel well enough to take the ride to return Chris to Tabor Academy after his winter break. It was a very quiet ride.

I was searching for words to say to our son, but all I could come up with was "Chris, I'm sure you know we're in for some tough times."

He nodded. "I know, Dad, but we'll be OK."

With that, I took a very lonely ride home, not knowing that four days later we would be attending her funeral. Jane died late on the night of January 6, 2004—Armenian Christmas. She was fifty years old.

Chris and I finally moved into the house three years later while he was on break from Boston University. I had hired a chef, Matthew Tatro, because Jane had been a great cook and I wanted Chris, when he visited from college, to eat the same food his mother had made for him.

In the course of having all of things I'd stored in a Miami warehouse moved to the Bahamas, I received an email from Naaman Forbes, who handled my taxes down there. Naaman was also a real estate broker who owned a stationary store, a gas truck, and an extermination company, and his email asked me to deposit $85,000 into his account to cover my taxes for my containers. I called Kevin Clemente and asked him if Naaman was on the level, and Kevin assured me he was.

I sent Naaman the $85,000, and he requested another $35,000, which I also sent. We moved in over a two-and-a-half-day period, and the customs guy was there, checking off the chairs, the beds—all the stuff for the house. When we finished, right before we were going back to Boston, Naaman called me and said, "Charles, I've got some money for you, some change left over from the move. I can meet up with you and give it to you."

We had lunch together, and Naaman asked if I wanted the money wired into my account or a check. I opted for a check, and because Naaman had a checkbook for all of his businesses, I figured that was safest.

He wrote me a check for $25,000, and I deposited into my account in Boston. One week went by, two weeks, and the money didn't show up in my account.

I called Naaman. "Where's my money?"

He told me that he would talk to the woman at the bank and she would make things right. Well, six months later, the money still hadn't been deposited in my account. I was down in the Bahamas and asked Naaman about it again, and I got the same answer: the woman at the bank was going to take care of it.

I said, "Let's go see the woman."

Naaman brought me to the bank. The woman apologized profusely and handed me $25,000 in cash. It had been bogged down in paperwork in Nassau. They used my money, interest free, for six months. That was, I learned, the local custom, whether for $25,000 or $25 million.

During the next six years, I spent between thirty and sixty days a year at my house in Emerald Bay. Chris brought his friends, and I brought mine. Mostly, I mourned and distracted myself with golf and buying up the lot to the right of me for $925,000 and the one to the left for $650,000. I planned to build a spec house and set up an offshore company to do it, which cost me about $300,000. Between my house and my other projects, I spent $7 million in the Bahamas before disaster struck.

Around 2012, a real estate downturn hit, and the Four Seasons moved out of the Bahamas. We lost all our amenities. The casino had closed earlier, and the marina had been poorly designed. I once saw a gorgeous 160-foot yacht with a giant hole in its nose from entering the channel, twisting sideways, and crashing into the sea wall.

Emerald Bay was a $375 million project, and Sandals, an all-inclusive resort, bought it for $27 million. All the lots that weren't sold now belonged to them, along with the marina and golf course. I unwound my position and lost most of my money. I didn't really miss the house after I left. After all, it had bookended the most painful years in my life.

# CHAPTER 17
# REGRETS ON MARLBOROUGH STREET

Not all of my father's plans panned out. In 1960, he bought 19 Marlborough Street, and ultimately 5, 7, 9, and 11, with an eye to knocking down those buildings and replacing them with a significant residential project. In retrospect, I can see that this was never going to happen. Because of their historical value, those buildings couldn't be torn down, and I doubted that my father ever had the capital or the ability to borrow the required funds to make his dream project a reality.

I suppose he could've looked for another location outside Back Bay—on Beacon Hill, for instance. Dad had done a lot of remodeling for Tom Diab there: Beacon Street, Myrtle Street, and Louis Berg Square. But he avoided Beacon Hill because he could never find a parking space for his car while he went into a property to work. Besides, my father thought Marlborough was the perfect street—quiet and gas-lit, and it was the first block by the public gardens so it was a prestigious address.

Everything my father bought was a fixer-upper. He told me that people usually inherited the townhouses from their wealthier parents or grandparents and would rent out rooms to help support it. Then they got old and tired, which was when he'd buy and start converting to apartments.

In the 1960s, 19 Marlborough Street was rented out as a rooming house. Each room had a hot plate, and the residents shared bathrooms. The house had what is known as a "New York entrance," straight in from the sidewalk, and the basement windows were big and waist high. The basement had a subbasement with a ten-foot-high ceiling. When I was in high school, my father sent me to 19 Marlborough to cut the two-by-four patch of grass in the front, and I soon graduated to doing building maintenance.

It bothered me that 19 was a rooming house. Each of the rooms went from $88 to a $100 a month. The residents kept to themselves. The house hadn't been remodeled. In the basement was a three-bedroom apartment we rented out to stewardesses. It stayed occupied for a dozen years. One stewardess would move out and another would move in.

On the first-floor front, a gentleman lived there with his wife. After she passed away, he lived there alone. I don't remember his name. He was big, clean-shaven, and stocky and always wore fine suits and ties. I tried to chat with him, but he was grumpy and would complain a lot. I didn't let it bother me. Every month he walked over to our office on Newbury to pay his rent. As the years went by, he couldn't walk up the office stairs anymore so he'd come to the front of our building and blow a whistle. Everyone in the office knew who it was, and someone would go down and collect his rent check.

One day, when I was cutting the lawn, a nurse walked by and asked, "Do you know of any rooming houses nearby?"

"This one right here," I said.

We had the first-floor rear room available—a huge room with a big, leaded, glass window overlooking the back with tall ceilings, French doors at the entrance, and a fireplace. I think there was also a sink in that room, and a small refrigerator. She lived there for many years. Every Christmas she'd call me and say, "Something's wrong in my apartment, and I left you a little bottle of cheer in the refrigerator."

I'd go in to find a half bottle of champagne.

On the third-floor front, there was a gentleman who must've been a retired army colonel. He owned a piano and a collection of hand-carved ivory antiques of monkeys and elephants and things like that in his apartment like you couldn't believe. It reminded me of an antique shop. He had his own bathroom as well. As the years went by, someone in the building had to call me because he was yelling from his apartment that he fell down and couldn't get up. I had to come over with the key and call the right people to help take care of him. He was alone.

As I tended to 19 Marlborough, it became clear that the property would earn more if we converted it from a rooming house. My father wasn't inclined in that direction, and I asked if I could buy the building from him.

"What?" he said. "Are you crazy? It's worth a million dollars."

After Dad died, my mother owned the building. By then, the residents had moved out, and the property needed a total overhaul. It never occurred to me to do it myself, and maybe transform it into a townhouse and move from 16 Exeter. I arranged to sell 19 for $1 million. The buyer went in and started renovating, but a couple of years later, the real estate market went through a tough period and he lost the property.

There are rare times when I second-guess decisions I've made in this business, and selling 19 Marlborough was one of them. I regret it very much. Presently, it's among the top five townhouses in Back Bay with a garage, outdoor parking, and a lap pool in the subbasement. It's estimated value is $35 million. It's a gorgeous, quality-built home with fine detail from top to bottom. For me, the building is like the girl who got away.

In the 1990s, Jane, Chris, and I would ski at Loon Mountain. We had a time-share with another family. The husband was my good friend, Dick Drinkwater. Dick introduced me to the guy who had bought 19 Marlborough Street. His name is Dean Stratouly, a big developer in Boston. His kids were up there skiing, and I said to Dean, "It's nice to meet you. You know, one of the sorriest things I ever did was sell that building."

And Dean replied, "One of the sorriest things I ever did was buy it."

I suppose it cost a small fortunate to maintain, yet I still wished that I'd bought it.

Another mistake I made in real estate was not as a buyer but as a broker. My father wanted to move his office to the first floor at 240A Newbury Street/39 Fairfield Street. (This was right before Tech HiFi showed up, and I convinced him to take the rental income instead.) Dad contacted a drapery-and-carpeting guy to set up the office. The guy worked out of Medford Center. Evidently, he inherited a warehouse on Route 128 and wanted to give me the listing. I had a great billboard sign made and put it out on his property. We start getting a burst of inquiries about it from buyers, and one afternoon the guy called me and asked how it was going.

"Great," I answered. "Lots of calls. But I don't think we'll get $250,000 for it."

His voice full of indignation, he snapped, "I told you $1,250,000."

I said, "Well, that just goes to show you. It's not selling for $250,000 either."

You often run into sellers with very unrealistic expectations in this business, and particularly in the current market. In the old days, you would be respectful and simply decline the offer to sell it for them. Today, unfortunately, brokers will give you high prices to get the listing. They figure, *OK, over time, I'm gonna show it and beat you down and sooner or later you'll get the price low enough to sell.* I try to avoid that type of thing.

Today, it also seems that many buyers shy away from the responsibility and effort of fixer-uppers. This generation of buyers doesn't want the bother of doing the work. I do believe there's a niche business, especially in Back Bay, for small fixer-uppers. It's a totally untapped business now for anyone who wants to roll up their sleeves.

Before I leave Marlborough Street, one final note: it will always remain at the center of my memory for one reason: fire.

In practice, I try not to overinsure our properties, and I do some self-insuring as well, because we keep up our buildings and watch them. And during the half century I've been in business, I've only had a handful of insurance claims. The claim on 5 Marlborough in the 1970s was the biggest and, potentially, the most tragic.

On New Year's Eve, the people on the top floor had a party. It must have been a real wingding because someone fell asleep in the living room. At one point, an ember dropped out of the fireplace and embedded itself between the hearth and the hardwood flooring, and apparently the ember had been smoldering below the floor all night. In the morning, when the reveler in the living room woke up, he couldn't see any flames, but he was choking on the smoke. The fire department was summoned. They had to chop out the ceiling from the apartment below to hose down the smoldering timbers. It was, to say the least, a mess, and in the end, repairs had to be made to all five floors of the building. In today's dollars, the claim was in excess of $200,000, and even now, decades after the incident, I'm grateful that the only thing that burned was our building.

3-5-7 Marlborough Street.

240 A Newbury Street.

9-11 Marlborough Street.

5-7 Marlborough Street.

Block of stores in Lynn, Mass.
My first lesson in local corruption.

240 Newbury Street, after our renovation.

1043-1045 Beacon Street. My father was a fan of assumable mortgages, so in in 1978 when he found these two, he bought them.

326 Dartmouth Street. In 1963 my father bought this property. It was a large, beautiful townhome on a wide corner lot and home to the German consulate.

1695-1697 Commonwealth Avenue, Alston. This was my first major investment in a building. It's where I learned how to undertake significant renovations and how to manage a property.

131 Coolidge Avenue, Watertown. To avoid any familial unpleasantness, Jane and I eloped on Friday, December 3, 1982, marrying before a judge at the courthouse in Cambridge. We lived in my two-bedroom condo in this high rise, right on the Charles River and overlooking the Boston skyline.

3 Union Park Square in the South End of Boston. I loved the building, but my timing was terrible. Prime rate hit 21 percent, never a happy situation for a developer in the middle of a condo project.

16 Exeter / 196-198 Marlborough Street, Boston. Jane and I found a lovely townhouse, built in 1910. It was a corner building with three entrances and had been built by a Dr. Bradbury, and I believe it was the first building in the United States where more than one dentist practiced together. The residential entrance was at 16 Exeter Street; the commercial entrances were at 196 and 198 Marlborough Street.

10 Williams Street, Watertown. I lived here prior to my marriage to Jane. Watertown was very affordable, and I had easy access to Boston driving down the Back River Road and onto Storrow Drive.

Jane, Chris, and I standing on the site of 29 Ockway Bay Road in Mashpee Mass. All I wanted was an escape from Boston in the summer. The problem was that I couldn't afford to buy a house with a view. So I found a partner to bid with me, and we won, paying $117,000 for 10 acres on the water. We put in the road, utilities, gas, water, and telephone and sold off the lots. In the end, he kept one for himself and I took the lot on the point.

The Newbury sign honoring my father.

215 Newbury Street, Boston.

176 Newbury Street, Boston.

222-232 Newbury Street, Boston.

222-232 Newbury Street, after our renovation.

905-907 Boylston Street, Boston. This was formerly a Chinese restaurant. I bought it in order to combine it with 907 and put up an eight-story building. But this plan has been tied up by the COVID pandemic for almost three years.

647 Boylston Street, Boston. I got a call. Do you want to buy this building? Why not, I thought, but I quickly realized that this block had a limited number of storefronts, so I just as quickly sold it off.

326 Cambridge Street, Boston. In 2000, I bought a hole in the ground with a completed permitted design and built it. A good location, across from Mass General Hospital, and I'd been looking for something to do. I put in two shops on the lower floor, and Mass General wound up leasing the upper floors. The Beacon Hill Civic Association wasn't happy about Mass General being there and had them sign a good-neighbor letter stating that the hospital wouldn't occupy any more space on the south side of Cambridge Street.

# CHAPTER 18
# FAMILY MATTERS

———◆———

When my sister Gail got married, she and her husband lived in the Fairview Avenue house in Belmont that our grandparents had given to her. Right before Gail's marriage, my father wanted to put the ownership of the house in a trust to protect my sister in the event the marriage didn't work out. Gail didn't agree, and my mother sided with Gail, so my father dropped it. A year or so later, my sister got divorced, and her lawyers made sure she wound up owning the property. That was when Gail put the house in a trust and lived there and collected rent from the other floor.

Gail remarried, and she and her husband, Richard O'Reilly, stayed in the house for many years until they bought a beautiful house in Winchester, a small suburban town five miles from Boston. They kept the Fairview two-family as an income property, and here is where the story gets a bit complicated.

When my grandfather was making arrangements to disperse his estate, he left my mother's sister and her husband a block of stores. There was also a two-family house behind it, and the block of stores across the street. That was for my aunt, Peggy Najarian, and her husband, Leo, who had worked in my grandfather's supermarket.

My grandfather came to see my mother and told her that he was going to leave the store and the two-family house behind the store to Peggy but that the four stores across the street were going to be left to my mother. That was great because my mother always supported my father's ideas, his money was always sunk in his properties, and they lived on a tight budget that didn't include much disposable income. With these properties, she'd be a landlady with her own money. It was a one-third to two-thirds split in favor of Aunt Peggy, but that was fine with my mother because my aunt and her family needed the money more than my mother did.

However, when my grandfather went back to tell the other side of the family about how his holdings were going to be divided, they were upset and thought that the properties should be kept together as a package, and they should inherit all of them. My father then spoke up, saying that his children had each received two-family houses from my grandfather and those properties should be added to the estate. Everything should be appraised to calculate the total value, thereby making it a simple matter to divide the estate into equal portions. I suspect my father knew what would happen when he suggested total fairness. They rejected his suggestion because they knew they had the best of the deal.

My poor grandfather! To keep the family peace, he needed another plan. He came back to talk to my mom in her kitchen in Belmont, telling her that instead of leaving her the building he was going to put $100,000 in a joint savings account with my grandmother, and when my grandmother passed away, the account would be my mother's. Under this arrangement, it was unclear whether she'd inherit much money at all, but in the interest of peace and to avoid hurting her father's feeling, my mother didn't argue for her rightful share. As it turned out—and further proof that no good deed goes unpunished—after my grandmother passed away, we heard rumblings that people suspected my mother of stealing the bank account.

And now the two-family on Fairview would play a role in shaping my family's future. Here's what happened.

One day, my father sold 314 Newbury Street to a man. Twenty years later, the man phoned me and asked if I'd like to buy the building back.

"Sure," I said.

When the deal was under agreement, I started thinking that 314 would be a good building for my sister. Gail still owned the two-family house on Fairview Avenue, and it was worth maybe $400,000 on today's market. I thought that 314 was a small building. I didn't need it, and Gail would do well owning it.

What I did then was what is known as a 1031 Exchange, which is a way to save on capital gains taxes by using two properties. The price for 314 Newbury was $2 million, and I used the Fairview house to pay for some of the building, which allowed Gail to delay paying taxes on the increased value of her house. I put 314 into tip-top shape for Gail, and she collected the rental income.

A few years later, I was looking at four buildings on Clarendon Street to buy for $8 million. I spoke to Gail, and we decided to do a 1031 Exchange on 314 Newbury. We sold it for $3 million and exchanged it for the four Clarendon Street buildings.

Because Gail has no children, she decided to put that transaction in my son Christopher's name. Chris made those buildings part of his company. They are valued at $15 million, and Gail receives a large paycheck for life.

Looking back at my experience with my mother's family and my sister, I suppose it would be fair to say that real estate can bring out the worst, and the best, in people.

# CHAPTER 19
# HOME

By the early 1990s, parking on Exeter Street had become a major inconvenience. We had a young child, and we were loading and unloading a stroller, a car seat, and groceries. Boston has parking garages, but they're often blocks away. I had to park behind one of the buildings, but Jane, who was always running here and there with Chris and doing all the additional errands required for handling the household, would have to park on the street with the residential parking sticker. That was getting harder and harder to do because there were far more parking stickers issued than there were parking spaces. To unload the car, she'd have to double park, and even though she wasn't blocking traffic, people would honk and shout at her. After a while, she was worn out with it.

We put 16 Exeter on the market, but no one wanted to buy the building with the residential and commercial rentals. They all wanted to buy our duplex as a condo unit—the second and third floors—which was about 9,000 square feet. Half of the potential buyers, I guessed, could have easily afforded the entire building, though none of them wanted to be landlords.

Meantime, we planned to escape to the suburbs by purchasing an old colonial house at 137 Marsh Street in Belmont, not far from an excellent private school, Belmont Hill. When we bought it, we were looking at it long term, thinking that we'd tear it down and build another house. Chris was seven years old. He had been in private school for kindergarten and first grade, and we thought Belmont Hill would be a good school for him. And we would have a garage and a driveway!

So now we owned the house in Belmont and Boston. We were stuck, not knowing what to do, and finally chose to put 16 Exeter on the market as a whole, and the house in Belmont. After one of them sold, we'd conjure up another plan.

The Belmont house sold first, and the buyer, whom I never met in person, turned out to belong to the same club as us on Cape Cod. We didn't make any money on the sale because we carried it for years, plowed the driveway, heated it, and paid the taxes.

The truth is I liked living in Boston and walking to my office, and suddenly we caught something of a break. At the building next to us—194 Marlborough Street—a lifetime parking spot became available and we bought it for $60,000. It was in a block of six spaces. You had to park in tandem with somebody else. This meant one was in front, the other was in back, and you'd have to swap keys or have a schedule. Not a perfect solution, but an improvement. Today, those spaces sell for $400,000, and you have to pay taxes on them and shovel the snow.

In looking over the paperwork for the sale, my lawyer spotted a problem. The spaces weren't supposed to be sold separately.

"But you do have title insurance," my lawyer said. "If it ever becomes an issue, you've got some protection."

Naturally, there was an issue. A couple from Rhode Island who lived in the tiny first-floor apartment of that building ended up selling their apartment to their daughter, who was starting out as a lawyer. She read the condo documents and realized that there was a parking space that was supposed to be included with the unit, and she didn't have it. It was the parking space we owned. She sued us. The title insurance company kicked in and paid for our attorney who was terrible and—to make a long story short—after numerous court appearances, we lost our space. Our legal fees were paid by insurance, and most of the money we paid for the space was returned. Even so, the process wasn't worth the aggravation.

On a Thursday summer afternoon, a broker whom I knew, Lois Kunian, showed me a building at 129 Commonwealth Avenue, an owner-occupied, six-unit property with six parking spaces in the rear that I saw as a disastrous money pit. It had a hot-air heating system, which is too dry for the New England cold—as opposed to old-fashioned cast iron radiators that give off residual heat—and a back staircase made of wrought iron and wood. The first-floor rear had cabinets painted black and a sleeping loft only a few feet from the ceiling. French doors were installed at the base of the first-floor entrance that led you up a dark, narrow hallway to the second floor. The top-floor rear apartment featured orange shag carpeting, but the top-floor front was decent. The building was terribly cut up. I envisioned it as a total-gut rehab, and I was tired just thinking about all the work. The asking price was $2 million, and I calculated that it would be about $1.2 million to fix—more than I wanted to pay.

I told Lois, "I'm tired of working. I'm tired of renovating. Thank you, but I'm not interested."

As I was walking out to go to Cape Cod for the weekend, there was another broker leading a client inside. When I got to the cape, I told Jane how horrible the building was. In my mind, it remained horrible until Sunday when I thought that perhaps I should renovate it because the location was excellent, it had the parking spaces, and it sat on the sunny side of Commonwealth Avenue, which is a fabulous street.

I shared my thoughts with Jane, and on Monday, I said, "Let's talk to the broker."

I called and discovered that the building was under agreement.

"Be in touch if the buyer changes his mind or the deal falls through," I said. "We want to close on it."

For whatever reason, the deal fell through. I agreed to a price of $1.8 million delivered vacant, and I was able to take my architect in and get some measurements so the plans would be ready and the building permit issued by the closing on January 6. We closed at ten in the morning, and by noon, contractors with sledgehammers were taking down the walls.

The building was transformed into a five-story, 9,000-square-foot townhouse with six parking spaces. Out of the eleven fireplaces, we maintained eight—all wood burning—which is allowed in Back Bay as long as you get the chimneys and flues checked, and we converted five to gas burning. In the basement were boilers and hot water tanks, the electrical and gas, and the panel boards, but the ceiling was low, less than five feet high. I figured it would be hard to get guys to do service work down there since they'd have to crouch until they were bent up like question marks, and because they often work while smoking cigarettes, I worried that they could blow up the basement. To address that problem, I had the boiler room dug out and fit with a nine-foot ceiling.

For the renovation, I used my architect, Guy Grassi, who had done many plans for me in Back Bay, and we had a solid working relationship. I checked on the progress every day because the house was only a block from my office. I told Guy, "I don't have a builder. I haven't done a big job like this in a long time."

Guy suggested I use these two brothers. They were doing some renovations on buildings on another block of Commonwealth Avenue. Guy took me over there to see them. The workmanship was excellent, the construction site was clean and organized, so I agreed to hire them after reaching an agreement on the price.

Unbeknownst to me and Guy Grassi, however, the two brothers had two separate companies, and I got the lousy company, which doesn't even work in Boston anymore. A lot of the workmanship was so bad I refused to pay the last payment of $110,000, and we wound up in court. The judge sent a professional to inspect the things we were arguing about, and the judge ruled in my favor. So I had $110,000 to spend on a new builder.

Once that was out of the way, the renovation, which lasted fourteen months, became a labor of love for me, and today, twenty-six years later, I still marvel at how the house turned out. I understand that while talking about it I can sound as tiresome as a parent bragging about a child. For me, this goes beyond the pride of creation or ownership. Buildings, to me, are art. I get the same aesthetic pleasure looking at them as the aficionados who ooh and aah at the paintings in the Museum of Fine Arts.

When you walk in, there is a gracious staircase going up to the second floor. You used to enter in the basement. There are French doors that open onto a little Romeo-and-Juliet-type balcony off the living room. In all of these old townhouses, the cooking was done in the basement on a cast iron stove. We put the kitchen on the third floor with the dining room. The second floor has the living room and my main study, which took six men six months to build. It is made of mahogany. The master bedroom takes up the entire fourth floor. The top floor has three more bedrooms, two more bathrooms, and a laundry room. There is a roof deck overlooking Commonwealth Avenue. I love to stand out there and admire the trees exploding in color during the fall or on clear nights in the winter when I can look at the Christmas tree lights twinkling below.

My decorator was originally from New England, but my mother found him in Florida and hired him to help with her condominium. I hired him, and the one instruction I gave him was that as the house aged, I wanted it to resemble the old Ritz-Carlton Hotel.

"I understand," he said. "You want shabby chic."

And that was exactly what we got. Some of the upholstery on the chairs that sit in the sun now have splits in them. The rugs have faded to a new kind of beauty. The large dining room, with its vaulted ceiling, lovely moldings, and fireplace, has a hushed elegance, and some friends refer to it as "Club Talanian."

The final act of moving in proved to be the most amusing. When I was transferring our main telephone number from Exeter to Commonwealth, I said to the operator at the phone company, "I've been paying $2.95 a month for the past twelve years to have an unlisted number and keep my name out of the phonebook."

"You don't have to do that," she said.

"What do you mean?" I asked.

She said, "Give me your name, but it doesn't have to be your real name. Just make one up, and then you won't have to pay the $2.95 a month."

I said, "I can tell you Mickey Mouse?"

"Sure," the operator said.

I gave her a name.

"What's your new address?" she asked.

I replied, "It's 129 Commonwealth Ave."

"Really?" she said. "I used to live there. On the top floor, the front apartment."

I said, "With the black-and-white diamond-shaped entry foyer into the kitchen?"

The operator said, "That's the one."

I said, "I'm so sorry for throwing you out."

And the operator laughed.

# CHAPTER 20
# THE CAPE

For thirty years, through ups and downs, the house on Ockway Bay Road in Mashpee was always a respite from the world, a place filled with summer light and joy. My son, his wife, and my two grandchildren, Celena and Charlie, liked to visit, and in memory, I can hear all of their laughter and see them out by the pool and on the deck. I began thinking that with all of our visitors, the house had become too small and we should buy a bigger place. Of course, I must admit, I take great pleasure in exploring real estate for sale, so even if I didn't find what I was looking for, I would enjoy the search.

While I was looking around, I happened to be speaking on the phone with one of my attorneys from Boston. He had a home on the cape and was the president of Oyster Harbors Golf and Country Club in Osterville. He invited me to join the club, and I said that I'd seen some property in Osterville, one of seven villages within the town of Barnstable and renowned for its quiet beauty and waterfront estates along Nantucket Sound. I knew Paul Fireman of Reebok and Bill Koch had places there. Koch bought his parcel of land from the Mellon Bank family for $22 million.

My application to Oyster Harbors was accepted. It was a beautiful, old club with an excellent golf course and good food. I looked at over a dozen homes on the island where the club was located, but the houses didn't have the same water views we had in Mashpee, where we could see the boats on the bay and water-skiers and kayakers—all sorts of activities to watch.

Now I noticed that this place at 132 South Bay Road was repeatedly being put on and taken off the market. I guessed that it was because the woman who lived there—the spry, eighty-five-year-old Mrs. Lane—was hesitant to leave for a smaller home. She had lost her husband about a decade ago. He was a builder in Framingham, Massachusetts, and this was their year-round home. They built it themselves on two acres of land, adding a tennis court and a country-club-sized, indoor swimming pool. It had its own beach and a permanent dock with no restrictions, which is hard to get. And a lot of the houses I looked at in Osterville had seasonal docks that had to be taken out every year and put back in. They have changed a lot of rules on the cape. You can't build that close to the water anymore, but the old places were grandfathered in.

I wasn't in a hurry because I was building in Florida, and I always had my house on the cape, even if it was too small to accommodate all of my guests. I spoke to the Realtor handling the property and said, "Why don't we look at the house and if we like it, we can make a deal and I could purchase it and let Mrs. Lane live there for two years?"

And that was exactly what happened. I looked at the house, negotiated a bit, bought it for $7 million, and wrote a two-year lease for a dollar that allowed Mrs. Lane to stay.

The bid-ready plans were completed by the time Mrs. Lane moved out in May 2019. The plans called for remodeling the existing house, tearing out the indoor swimming pool, and building another house in that space. The house we built in that space would be attached to the old house and its three-car garage, which had a two-bedroom apartment above it. But the bids to do the work were astronomical, and the builder said it would be cheaper to tear the house down and start fresh. That was what I did, though I kept the garage.

The new house would be built farther back from the waterline, which saved us a lot in mitigation fees. For every foot you're in the mitigation area, you have to plant nine square feet. The conservation commission doesn't let you plant in the front of your house or in the sides. They want you to plant right in front of your view of the water. That's the logic of conservation. If they deem you're doing something environmentally unsound, you have to pay for it. The plantings they make you put in hold the ground together so it doesn't wash away the natural habitats of birds, bees, and other wildlife.

It didn't bother me to pay $7 million for a house I was tearing down, but the mitigation money bothered me because it felt as if I were getting my pocket picked. I was being unreasonably forced into it. My waterline in Mashpee—I'm on a point and there's a marsh on one side and water on two sides—hadn't changed in thirty years. Nothing has—not my tree line, my shore, or my little beach. Nothing. I do believe we might be having some global warming and tides are higher than before, and ice may be melting. But we went through an ice age and maybe we'll go through a warming age. And maybe we'll go through an ice age again.

The Obama Administration took $23 billion out of a fund designated for floods and disasters. How are we going to pay it back? By moving the flood line on all the maps and sticking the people who weren't in flood zones before into one and forcing them to pay drastic increases in their flood insurance.

I avoided that by moving the house back ten or twelve feet so I wasn't planting 3,000 square feet of brush that would've blocked the view of the water. Now the pool is between the back of the garage and the new house. You can see Nantucket Sound from there. We're on what's known as Little Island on the sound. Along that street are probably six houses facing south to the waters of West Bay. The house was finally finished in the spring of 2021.

Entering through the front door of the house and going straight, you see the water. Walking into the living room, you've got your fireplace to the right in the living room. If you stand at that fireplace, you will be looking at a wall of glass and out to the water. It's going to go from a double living room to a bar, kitchen, dining room, and a TV room—all glass looking out the back of the house. I'm excited about that because looking at the water is a wonderful way to relax.

My greatest thrill is watching the construction process. I love paying attention to the details. For example, when I walk into a room, I ask myself where the light switch should go to be most convenient. With guest rooms, you want to make it as simple as possible. The same goes for the placement of the outlets and mirrors and door handles on the closets. A guest should be able to use a room without consulting a chart.

Whatever you are going to spend building a house, you want to make certain that you get precisely what you want. There are people who just want to buy a fancy place they can bring their friends to to show them how much they can spend. That's not me. I didn't have to do this. I could have stayed in Mashpee. But as a child, I liked taking things apart to see how they worked, and this house is the grown-up version of that.

In addition, a nice home—regardless of price—has always been important to me. It was important to my grandparents and parents, and I noticed that it seemed to be a priority among Armenians. I suspect that is because family was most central, and houses were where your family lived and spent most of their time.

So I have come to understand that for me my love of tinkering and my desire to be surrounded by the blessings of family have converged, and I can see both any time I look at a house I've designed and built.

# CHAPTER 21
# A MOST UNUSUAL FELLOW

———— •◆•◆• ————

Tom Brennan, who was a broker in my office for thirty-six years, had been trying to sell 254 Newbury Street for the gentleman who was a longtime owner of the building. This fellow operated his business there and knew my father quite well. Finally, Tom sold 254 to a couple who had their business and lived in the building. Then when the economy nosedived, it hurt their business and they decided to sell. Tom worked on the building for over three months to make a deal. His potential purchaser was Mouldi Sayeh.

When it came time for Mouldi to purchase the building, he had to delay closing. His father had passed away, and he returned to his native Afghanistan for the funeral. Evidently, he hadn't arranged financing because when he came back to Boston, Tom brought him to me. I was about to leave for the Bahamas and really had no time for a meeting, but Tom said that Mouldi was desperate and I have a soft spot in my heart for real estate buyers who are squeezed for financing—a condition I understand—so I met with him.

Mouldi was very short and very dark, with fleshy features, and he was wearing a camel-hair overcoat. He was exceedingly polite and asked if I would lend him $1 million—half the money he needed—to buy 254 Newbury. He owned two condominiums across the river in Cambridge that he could use as collateral. There were no mortgages on them, and they were valued at $1.5 million.

I said, "Mouldi, this is a faceless loan. In other words, this is a business deal. I accept your collateral. It's all about the buildings. I'm going to loan you the money. I don't know you. You don't know me. But let me tell you something. If I don't get paid, I'm taking your property."

I call it a faceless loan because it's strictly business so I operate in this deal in as hardcore a manner as a bank. I didn't know if Mouldi was an American citizen, and I didn't care. All I knew was that I had three pieces of property in the United States, and I'm the first name on the deed. So if Mouldi didn't pay me, I would be covered. I wouldn't even call him about it. I didn't ask him for an application, and I didn't even have his phone number. I just said, "Sure," because I know I have the property as collateral.

Normally, in a regular mortgage, the person's credit, financial status, and payment history would be checked. In my "faceless" loan exchange—a term I made up—all I check on are the value of the buildings so my money is guaranteed. I was loaning him $1 million and getting $3.5 million worth of collateral, so I was golden. It was about property, and for me, it underscored how lucky I was to have the cash to do this kind of a deal—a deal that I wouldn't even have dreamed of in my early days in real estate.

Mouldi paid me every month as he was supposed to. If I walked by him on the street as he was sweeping the sidewalk in front of the building, he'd bring me inside and show me around. At Christmastime, he'd give me a bottle of wine. He used to call me Mr. Charles. He'd hold his hands together, like he was praying, and nod his head. We got to know each other from being neighbors on Newbury Street, and we became friends. He finally paid me off a few years later—I wasn't charging him an exorbitant amount of interest—and I didn't see him again for a long time.

Some years later, Mouldi called me wanting to come into the office. We met up, and he asked, "Do you know this man: Bill Haney?"

I was immediately on high alert, and I told Mouldi that I'd had a run-in with Haney. Back then, Haney called my office and told my receptionist that he was a neighbor of mine on Cape Cod in Mashpee. I'd recently bought property there and planned to subdivide some of it and build a house on the remaining lot. I was excited that Haney called and thought it was nice that a neighbor would want to come and see me because I'd always dreamed of having a house and a life on Cape Cod.

When Haney entered my office, he appeared quite angry and demanded to know what I was going to do with the property.

I remained polite and replied, "I'm going to subdivide it and build a house."

I don't know if he liked the answer, but he left.

Anyway, when Mouldi mentioned him, I had a feeling there was a problem.

"What's going on, Mouldi?"

It turned out Mouldi was delinquent on a loan to a bank. Now Bill Haney is one of the bottom-feeders you find in the real estate game. They call up banks and ask if there are any delinquent loans for sale. So for instance, if the bank has a $300,000 mortgage they no longer want, they will sell it to the bottom-feeder for $250,000, and he starts going after the debtor as if he's guilty of a high crime.

Haney had bought Mouldi's mortgage, and he kept phoning him, saying, "You owe me money. You have three months' back payment you haven't made."

I didn't know why Mouldi hadn't paid the bank, but I felt terrible that Bill Haney was giving him such a hard time.

"Mr. Charles, Mr. Charles," Mouldi said. "Can you help me?"

"My guess is Haney's going to foreclose on you, and you'll lose the building. Why aren't you paying him?"

I don't remember the reason Mouldi gave me. Nor do I know how long Haney owned that mortgage, but that was probably the fastest money he ever made. I think I loaned Mouldi over $1 million because I'd had a good experience with him before, and frankly, because I didn't like Bill Haney. Now I had a new first mortgage on the property, and I again received the condos in Cambridge for collateral so I felt secure.

Unfortunately, Mouldi stopped paying me. Maybe his business went bad or maybe his investors in Afghanistan had stopped funding him. I never discovered why he defaulted, and I didn't ask. I was told that he entertained Osama bin Laden when he visited the United States. I don't know whether Mouldi was involved with bin Laden or not, and I felt it was better that I didn't know about his personal history.

I was forced to foreclose on Mouldi. I started the process with local attorneys, and during the course of this, Mouldi decided to file bankruptcy, which he was entitled to do. This made the time it took to foreclose even longer, but I didn't care because the delay was paid for at an accelerated interest rate—18 percent, to be exact—and I knew that I would also be able to sell the property. The whole process took eighteen months.

I remember being in the judge's chambers, and Mouldi brought two potential buyers to bid on the property. Out in the hallway, I spoke to one of the potential buyers. His name was Bruce Percelay. (He lives in Back Bay now and invests in real estate.) Bruce asked me what I thought the building was worth.

I said, "If you bid $2.8 million, you'll own it because I know the other guys won't go that high. I'm guessing his budget is about $2.5 million."

The bids were put in envelopes and handed to the judge. When the judge opened them, Bruce was the high bidder at $3.4 million. The other bid was under $2.8 million. Bruce could've had it for $2.8 million, but he didn't believe me. Years later, he put it up for sale because was losing money on it, so I bought the building and remodeled it.

I never found out the whole story about Mouldi. And I never heard from him again. I heard that he was still in the United States and owned an antique shop somewhere in a suburb.

I do believe that his troubles started when his father had died, who I suspect was investing with him. That loss forced his hand to do a faceless deal with me rather than wait to complete the closing process for the $1 million through a bank. I do know that he left town at that time. I feel like I can read people pretty well and it didn't set off any warning bells for me because I've seen these deals before. Also, the collateral was so good that I couldn't lose.

That's really the name of the game in real estate. If you don't have money, then you have real estate. Like my father always said, "There's money in those bricks."

# CHAPTER 22
# FINALLY, MY PLACE

—◆•◆•◆—

As a child, I often thought, *I don't have a country. I don't have a place.* My Italian and Irish friends could go to Italy and Ireland, but where could I go?

My maternal grandmother Simonian had emigrated from Armenia, and I used to ask her, "How'd you get to America?"

And she'd say, "We came in a covered wagon."

I knew that wasn't true. I knew that her husband, my grandfather, had also immigrated to the United States, and when he arrived, he worked in a leather mill and a wire mill before he opened his grocery store.

My parents spoke Armenian. It was my first language, and when I three years old, I remember my mother saying to my father, "Charles is going to be starting school soon. We better drop the Armenian."

The mentality back then was that you're in the United States so you had to become an American and speak English, and I was never even given any ethnic food in my lunchbox. It was bologna sandwiches.

I can only remember hanging around with family. No outsiders. You knew your neighbors, but you didn't socialize with them. And in those days, your aunts and uncles, your grandmother and grandfather, they were all stand-ins for your parents. If they told you to do something, you did it.

My parents belonged to the Armenian Holy Trinity Church on Brattle Street in Cambridge. My grandfather was the godfather of the church, and my father was a trustee and on the building committee. On the day my father died, the priest came to his house, offered his condolences, and told us a story. My father was going to make a big donation to name the church hall and redo it. We were stunned. We usually knew what my father was doing. I talked it over with my family and the priest, and we decided to go through with Dad's plan, and today their church has the Charles and Nevart Talanian Cultural Hall.

All the Armenian churches in the Boston area shared a picnic ground: Camp Ararat in Maynard, Massachusetts. There was a big, grass field for a parking lot, a lake, buildings for a kitchen, another one for beverages, and an area for barbecuing. We'd go there after church, and someone would sell balloons and trinkets for the kids. You could get shish kebab or Armenian hamburgers, and the adults could get beers. They had Armenian music and dancing. It was like a brief trip back to the old country.

In 1991, Armenia declared its independence from the Soviet Union, and four years later, when I visited and traveled the country with two busloads of tourists, it looked like someone had blown the lunch whistle and everyone had left. There were construction sites with cranes sitting still and factories with conveyor belts, loaded with boxes, that weren't moving.

We stayed at the Hotel Armenia. It was located on Lenin Square, a five-lane roundabout, in the capital city of Yerevan. The hotel was one city block. I'm guessing it had 195 rooms, approximately 500,000 square feet. The architecture was Russian. The room was taller than it was wide, the little sconces were high on the walls, and the chandelier was very small and hung very high in keeping with the standards of Russian architecture, which was designed to make the government look big and the people look small.

They ran that hotel with five hundred people, mainly to provide jobs and to keep an eye on the guests. Floor ladies were stationed at each elevator twenty-four hours a day. You'd get off the elevator, and they'd give you your key. When you left your room, you'd give the key back to them and take the elevator downstairs. There was a doorman at the front door and a doorman at the back door. I held onto my key and made the floor ladies quite unhappy.

In 1997, the government was selling off assets. They were privatizing the airport. They sold the Armenian brandy factory to the French company Pernod Ricard. (To this day, they still make the brandy according to the old recipes, and it's terrific.) And when they decided to privatize the Hotel Armenia, Nishan and Kevork Atinizian wanted to buy it. I knew Nishan, and he asked to invest to the tune of $1 million, a lot of money now and even more over twenty years ago.

It sounded like a nutty idea. Then I thought about it for a few days. My sister Gail belonged to some Armenian groups that were active in the country's affairs and trying to help them recover from its Soviet past. I asked my accountant if I could afford to lose a million dollars. He said yes, so I asked my mother if she thought we should invest in the hotel. She liked what Gail was doing, and in the end, as a family, we invested with three other majority owners: the two Atinizian brothers, the Talanian family, and Carolyn Mugar, whose father had founded the Star Market chain of supermarkets in New England.

We paid $10 million for the hotel, the financing supplied by the US government, and probably sank another $12 million into it. I visited thirty or forty times while the renovations were going on. Armenia was a land-locked country, and you had to bring almost all of the materials from other countries: wire, pipes, boilers, air conditioners, etc. You name it, we had to import it.

We kept a lot of the employees that were with the hotel. By and large, Armenians are hard workers. Paying them was a struggle because the government operates so slowly. Nishan and I decided in order for the project to go smoothly, we had to use our own money and write the checks personally, and then submit requisitions to the government to get repaid. Nishan and I were writing checks to suppliers all over the world. My bank even called and asked me what I was doing.

The workers didn't always have the tools and equipment that they needed. I remember one guy doing plaster up on a scaffold, about fourteen feet high up on the wall. He was wearing two different shoes, an old Sunday white shirt, and pants that were too big for him with a rope belt. And the scaffold was lashed together with rope. In the United States, the Occupational Safety and Health Administration (OSHA) would've shut down the job in a heartbeat.

During the renovations, we discovered a secret club behind a panel door. The room had a billiard table, a bar, and a stage. We believed it had been a hangout for Soviet big shots. One of our doormen was the billiards champion in the area, so we donated the table to his club, which delighted him to no end. We also discovered a fake floor between the third-floor ceiling and the fourth floor. This was where the KGB had installed its listening devices. In fact, all the rooms in the hotel were bugged. We made good use of that phony floor by running our air-conditioning ductwork through it.

Today, Marriott operates the hotel, and we still own it. Even though we haven't made a profit, I'm proud of what we have accomplished. We set out to help people, and help them we did. When we arrived, the employees were living in cold water flats, and the work we provided improved living standards, and very few quit. Our employees work for Marriott. The hotel chain has done an excellent job training them and teaching most of them English. Their technical and language skills enable the employees to move around the world and still work for Marriott, going to countries that offer a better education for their children and a better life for their families.

Some partners want to sell the hotel; others want to keep it. For me, as I often feel about real estate, it's time to move on, and I'm hopeful we can find an Armenian group or individual to buy it. That would be a perfect ending.

# CHAPTER 23
# THE ABSURDIST
# OVERSEERS

⬥

South Cape Village in Mashpee was a commercial property across from Mashpee Commons. It started to come about when I bought a small building on Falmouth Road. It was a liquor store and condominium. It was one building out of two on an acre of land. The gentleman who sold it to me owned a lot of real estate in Chinatown, and he owned some acreage surrounding this particular parcel. Next to it was Dick and Ellie's Flea Market. They had the market, a miniature golf course, and a refreshment stand.

That was thirty years ago, and after I bought that building, which was called the Liquor Warehouse, I ended up buying the two- or three-acre parcel to the side of it as well as the two- or three-acre parcel behind it and another small parcel to the left. It had frontage on Route 28 and in the back, and frontage on Great Neck Road South. On the property, it had a pathway called Donna's Lane, which went from Great Neck Road South to Route 28. It was kind of like a corner. When I was on the cape, every weekend, I'd start my day by getting coffee down at the flea market, and I'd follow Dick Wasil around while he collected his $5 and $10 from every vendor renting a table.

I became friendly with Dick, and fifteen years later, he sold me the property. Now I owned close to twenty acres on two road frontages and Donna's Lane, which could be turned into a street. It's actually the parcel I should have put the brakes on because I was selling 19 Marlborough Street, which I liked, but I was depending on the proceeds from the sale of that building to buy the flea market.

Shortly after that, I received a letter from a gentleman in Cotuit who did permitting. This was a larger property and anything over 10,000 square feet requires you to go before the Cape Cod Commission to get its approval to proceed.

I'd been through the approval process with the Back Bay Commission in Boston, which was about as pleasurable as a double root canal. Believe it not, the Cape Cod Commission was worse—like having all your teeth pulled without Novocain.

It was apparent, from my first encounter with the cape commission, that they weren't there to help you; they're overseers and tree huggers who think they're smarter than they are, and they don't even have a registered architect on their board. Their overall philosophy about building something is animated by one absurd idea: when you're done building, you should have less traffic than what was in the area before. There are big developers with excellent reputations and deep pockets who want to do something on the cape and make it both aesthetically pleasing and profitable. But then they have to answer to these idiots whose basic attitude is "Stay out of my backyard," a position that will not find many friends among developers.

The Cape Cod Commission meets in a courtroom with a judge, and at one of the meetings, they were taking a vote on my plans when the senior member commented, "You know how I feel about this project. I don't like it and I'm not voting for it. But if you can get that piece of property, then I'll vote for the project."

The piece of land, which he described as the hole in the donut, was for conservation. ENSTAR, a natural gas company, owned it, and I worked for another six months to get the company to sell me that. It cost me about an acre of land that I had on route 28 in Mashpee plus $150,000. I went back to the commission and let the members know I'd bought the hole in the donut. And wouldn't you know? The senor member still voted against it. It was very discouraging. Meanwhile, I was mitigating traffic seventy-five to one hundred miles away from my site—installing a stop sign, painting a crosswalk—and paying for everything. I even did a complete lit intersection in Mashpee, which cost me a $1 million.

I hired a permitting gentleman by the name of Don McGathlin who was from Cotuit, and it took him nine years of putting the paperwork together, working with the traffic-counter guys, and working with the zoning board to permit South Cape Village. By the time I got permitted, I was probably into the project for over $3 million.

Originally, the design was for an off-price retail center that a company called Chelsea CGA owned. The company told me that if I built it, they would triple net lease it.

So I designed it that way, a total of 170,000 square feet. Yet when I was finally permitted to do it, we went back to Chelsea CGA, which had grown by leaps and bounds as a company. They informed me that that they didn't do anything under 350,000 square feet.

If it had taken eight months to a year, which is a normal permitting time, they would have rented it. We would have had a triple net lease with them. It would have been operating fully occupied, and it would have been a draw to that area of Mashpee because of the discount mode. But the Cape Cod Commission wanted the building to look like a Parisian park from the street. They wanted lots of landscaping, and I had dual sidewalks down on 28 and then up the hill parallel to the land—because it was slightly elevated—and they wanted all the parking in the back so it wasn't seen from the street.

Then a broker came along and brought us a tenant, Roche Brothers, a high-end, family-owned supermarket chain that wanted 40,000 square feet. But that much space in the off-price mall represented roughly twenty to forty tenants, where they're just one. Then they turned around and said, "Well, we like that, but we want to face the parking lot."

That was just the opposite of the Cape Cod Commission's rules. I needed a big tenant and took that chance. Roche Brothers went and got their designs approved to have their truck docks, loading docks, dumpsters, and compactors facing the street.

From there, I was able to continue going forward with permitting and building out the other 130,000 square feet originally planned for the mall. We got Marshalls as a tenant and, again, they wanted to face the parking lot. So we had Roche Brothers facing in one direction and Marshalls facing in another direction. Eventually, I was able to sign up Santander Bank, Olympia Sports, Game Stop, Walgreens, Dunkin' Donuts, a drycleaner, a mattress store, and a liquor store, but there was still a 14 percent vacancy. That nice, little walkway down the middle of the off-price retail center that was going to be filled with all kinds of little shops and a fountain and benches never got leased.

One story I'll never forget was that after I built the Walgreens, the Cape Cod Commission said that the side walls were massive and I should put some billboard frames up so pictures could be displayed there. Lighted glass shadowboxes went up on the walls, and Walgreens put pictures in them of a pharmacist passing out a prescription to a customer. It was a very friendly picture, but because the posters said Walgreens in the right-hand corner, the town deemed it as signage and ordered me to take it out.

Thus, the large shadowboxes were empty and looked stupid, and you would've been better off seeing bricks or shingles instead of blank advertising space.

Securing tenants on the cape is like pushing string; it just piles up in front of you and buckles under. I decided to get out and sold South Cape Village for a $5 million loss. I suppose when you take into consideration the depreciation and the tax write-offs, I made money.

But one thing for sure: I learned my lesson about developing on the cape.

# CHAPTER 24

# ANN

⸺•⟡•⸺

By December 2007, I'd been a widower for four years. I had dated on and off, but nothing serious enough to end the loneliness I felt in the aftermath of Jane's death.

Carol, who worked in my office, had planned our annual company Christmas dinner at the old Ritz-Carlton in Boston. I arrived at the dinner a little early, and Carol introduced me to Sherry, the woman who had helped her organize the dinner.

Sherry and I shook hands and said hello before she and Carol walked off to another part of the room. Evidently, Sherry asked Carol if I was single. Carol said, "Yes, but you better go over and talk to him before the rest of the office shows up."

Sherry came back and shook my hand again, asking me several serious questions that made me uncomfortable, because I thought she was going to ask me out on a date.

I was close. She wanted to know if she could fix me up.

I was relieved and said, "Sure, go ahead."

Sherry had just met Ann through a friend, and she introduced me to her. Ann was a pretty, blonde woman with a lovely smile, and a week or so later, I took her to dinner at the Mistral Restaurant. Ann had grown up outside Boston, and she was divorced. Her grandparents had had substantial real estate holdings in Brookline and Newton. When I was young, I used to drool over the Sunday paper seeing the buildings they owned. At the time of our dinner, I was working on building a bank at South Cape Village, and most of the evening was dedicated to talking about that. Not the most romantic conversation, which may be why no sparks flew.

Still, we liked each other enough to get together twice a year for a lunch and a dinner. On May 13, 2008, Ann was having a party for her birthday with some girlfriends. They planned to meet at Mistral for dinner, but first they were having drinks at Davio's. Ann invited me to stop by, which I thought was nice of her, so off I went to Davio's. Her best friend, Rana, was there and interrogated me about my family values, thoughts on children, and dating history as though she were running her own version of match.com. I finished my drink, picked up the tab for their round, and left. A smart move because I was afraid I'd get the wrong answer to one of her questions.

I liked Ann, but I didn't feel that we were getting along. I think she thought I was too harsh in my views. I'm protective of my family and the people around me. I can come off as extreme. I'm fully on one side or the other, almost never in the middle. But I don't show a lot externally. I'm more of a listener. I get the pulse of what's going on by listening. Some people spend so much time talking that all they hear are themselves. Which is like being your own psychiatrist.

In 2009, Ann bumped into my son on Boylston Street. My son had been working at a TV show, *Style Boston*, and they were holding a party at the Institute of Contemporary Art down on the Boston waterfront. I invited Ann, and it was almost a date. We had a nice time, but still I had the sense that Ann wasn't interested in me.

I have a good friend named Joan. We've known each for thirty-five years, and I didn't know it but Joan was one of Ann's close friends. So one day they were talking, and Joan told Ann she wanted to fix her up with somebody and mentioned my name.

"I've already been out with him a few times," Ann said. "No thanks."

Ann told Joan that we had a very different way of looking at things. Putting it mildly, I wasn't as flexible in discussion as she might like, and Joan, bless her heart, jumped to my defense, saying, "You've got the wrong guy. You're not reading him right. I've known Charles for a long time. You two have the same family and personal values. He's a good man. You're just not seeing him clearly."

Later, in the summer of 2009, I bought a new boat: a thirty-nine-foot Intrepid. I asked Ann if she'd like to visit and take a ride down the Cape Cod Canal. She agreed, and we had a wonderful little cruise. We kept up with our twice-a-year get-togethers, meeting for a quick drink, lunch, or dinner. As Ann continued to date, her friends Rana and Joan would occasionally bring me up to her, suggesting that she reach out or reconsider seeing me. They said that she might question her own snap judgment about me because maybe, just maybe, she wasn't seeing me correctly,

Rana and Joan must've convinced her because in the summer of 2012, we spent more time together, and Ann actually came to my house on the cape for weekends. We were kind of dating, but what was nice was that we were building a friendship first. Ann would come to visit, and we spent our days together talking by the pool or taking boat rides or five-mile walks to get a coffee, and we would wander around the little center with its shops or go out dinner with friends of mine.

At some point in September, Ann broke up with me. She was running a company, didn't have time to build a realtionship, and disappeared from my life. I remember one morning sticking a $20 bill in my sock when I went for a walk on our usual route to get coffee. I put the $16 and coins in my sock for the walk home, and when I got to the house, the only thing in my sock was the change. The bills were gone, and I felt very bad about it. Of course, I actually felt terrible about losing Ann, and whenever I went for coffee, I used to check the bushes for the missing money. Who knew? Maybe Ann would be hiding there as well.

My loneliest year was 2013. In June, my son Chris got married. I didn't have anyone special to take to the wedding and ended up bringing a woman I was dating in Florida. It was more like a semidate because she stood off to a side for much of the time because I didn't want people coming over to us and taking any attention away from my son and daughter-in-law's wedding.

By September 2014, I decided the hell with it and called Ann for a date. She agreed to go with me. I picked the Four Seasons because it was quiet and romantic and it would be easy to talk privately. As usual, I arrived early and sat by myself thinking, *This is a stupid idea. Why did you call her? This is never gonna work. You've been seeing her for over five years. Get it through your head. It doesn't work.*

I suppose it was my loneliness that made me speak more emotionally, and Ann liked that. I not only thought she was pretty, but I admired her. Ann was diligent and energetic. She was working at a venture capital company, in charge of forty people who raised capital in the financial field, and grew the company by leaps and bounds. She understands business in a different way than I do because she knows an awful lot about management and how to do things inside a real corporate structure. I'm more homegrown, and I've never really had a job in the traditional sense.

That fall with Ann was a joy. She also lived in Back Bay. We were going out on a date one day, and to get ready for the date, Ann went to the manicurist on the way to meeting me. She was rushing to get ready and change from her business outfit to her date outfit, and at the salon, she took out her jewelry. As she was putting on her diamond earrings, they brought her the bill for the manicure. When she went to pay her check, she put her earrings down on the counter, paid the bill and left, forgetting that her earrings were still on the counter. When Ann got home she realized it, and we rushed back to the shop and the earrings were gone.

Unlucky for Ann, but lucky for me. Valentine's Day was approaching, and I went to my jeweler, bought her another pair of diamond earrings, and picked out a nice-sized engagement ring just in case things headed in the right direction. I put the ring in the safe at home and brought the earrings with me for our dinner on Valentine's Day. Ann was very appreciative; I think she brings out the romantic in me. Our relationship was going well, and I doubt that either of us had ever been happier. That Christmas, we were still seeing each other, and Ann went out and got these baseball caps embroidered with the years of our dates. On the front of the hats, it said, "Let's talk about it."

Shortly after Christmas, Ann and I were going to go to the movies. I knew that she'd be leaving for London on business for a couple of weeks, and I had to be in Armenia because of the hotel renovation. By that point, Ann and I had discussed getting married a few times, and before I went to meet her, I took the ring out of the safe just in case the subject of marriage came up.

The movie theater was on Tremont Street, and we went to the Italian restaurant next door, El Trattoria, after the show. We were sitting there, talking about our plans again, so I put the ring on the table and asked her to marry me. She said yes, and after that, we went to have a glass of wine at the Four Seasons and decided it would be a nice place to get married. Now every time I mention going to eat at El Trattoria, Ann responds, "No way. Every time I go there I get engaged."

That is Ann—always making me laugh.

On September 7, 2014, we had a Jewish-Armenian wedding at the Four Seasons. Ann had done a lot of research on interdenominational weddings and ways to make everyone more comfortable. As I mentioned, Ann's very funny, and when we met with the priest and rabbi and discussed the ceremony, Ann had already come up with a few pages of jokes. She brought the jokes to our meetings and asked the clergymen if they could "say something like 'Have you heard the one about the rabbi and the priest in the Four Seasons?'" Initially they both said no, but they took all the punch lines she wrote up, and wouldn't you know it? Both the priest and the rabbi came through and did some comedy between the blessings. It was the best wedding ever. Everyone loved it!

There were about 125 guests at the reception. Ann's father was there, but her mom had passed away. Her mom had been sick for some time. They had been extremely close. Ann felt the most important thing was to be by her mom's side, and Ann had taken time off from working to be with her during her last years. I was impressed that she not only was with her but that she was financially responsible and had prepared herself financially to take care of herself for a number of years to put her mom first. It was a tough loss for Ann, but one benefit to marrying me is Ann's relationship with my mother. Ann is very appreciative to have Nevart in her life. She feels blessed to have her as her mother-in-law. They love each other. Ann is remarkably kind, and this isn't simply the judgment of a lovestruck husband. I can't tell you how many people have asked me, "Where'd you find her? She's the kindest person I've ever met."

Yes, she is. Ann is always saying, "Let's go visit or call your mom, your sister, your family, and friends."

For Ann, keeping my relationships close is extremely important, which is a good reminder for me.

Ann is a great fit for me in so many ways, but one in particular is her knowledge of how difficult it is to succeed, including how much work is required to reach your goals.

She is also remarkably—and verbally—appreciative. Probably a week doesn't go by that Ann doesn't say to me, "Thank you for this wonderful life you've provided for us."

Ann provides as well. She helped design our houses on the cape and in Florida. And she has such an in-depth knowledge of the stock market, which has become especially important lately. I've only been in bricks and mortar. Ann has guided our investment strategy, along with a friend of mine who acts as investment adviser, and we've made out quite well.

To this day, Ann and I talk about the long road we took to marriage. I have to thank her girlfriends Joan and Rana for helping Ann understand who I really was because she didn't figure it out on her own.

For so many years, I never thought I would be happy again. I'm grateful that Ann proved me wrong.

# CHAPTER 25
# A NEW BEGINNING

When Ann and I bought our home on West Key Palm Road in Boca Raton, we went through the punch list of what you have to do to become a Florida resident. We had to register to vote, get our driver's licenses, find doctors, join a church and clubs—all the things that make you a solid resident of a state. My goal was tax savings. Unlike Massachusetts, Florida has no state income tax. The savings for my estate would be significant so I decided to begin relocating some of my investments.

The building that I bought to celebrate my fiftieth birthday, 7 Newbury Street, had cost $4.8 million. It was running well. All the rents were at fair-market value, and all the leases were set. After all expenses, with no mortgage, the building returned $850,000 a year. That's a lot of money, but because the value of the building was now $26 million, the return was 3 percent.

I knew I could do better in Florida now that I was a resident. I had $26 million to spend on a 1031 exchange, which is where you sell and exchange one property for another and don't have to pay taxes on the increased value. A 1031 has specific rules, and it must be executed in a timely manner, no holding onto your profit while you leisurely make up your mind. I found a buyer for 7 Newbury who was willing to do the exchange, so Ann and I went looking.

Buying in Florida was a challenge for me because I knew nothing about the market. I have friends, Marta and Jimmy Batmasian, who own most of the retail in Boca Raton, and I'd had a bad experience with South Cape Village Shopping Center, so I decided to stick to offices.

The new office buildings I saw had nice fountains outside and beautiful lobbies. But I'd look around and saw that the only place you could go for lunch was the Chili's down the street. Which wasn't what I'm used to. Other office buildings would be five or ten miles from the coast of Boca, and they were lovely except for their high vacancy rates. I remember a set of two buildings the broker showed me, but they were owned by two different people, and that could be a terrible arrangement if you disagreed with the other owner about upkeep. In other words, a problem with one building could impact the rents on the other one.

At last, we saw Peninsula Executive Center, two buildings with a four-story aboveground garage and beautiful landscaping. The center was part of an office park, convenient for people commuting to work. What I liked about it most was that it was on Glades Road, so it had its own exit on the highway, and it was right down the street from Town Center, one of the area's largest malls; I noticed that even during tough times, the mall was upping its game. It was also directly across the street from Abe and Louie's Steakhouse. I knew Charlie Sarkis, the developer and original owner of Abe and Louie's. Abe Sarkis was Charlie's father, a bookie in Boston, and I remember the day he got out of jail. Sarkis decided to be legitimate, and he went into the real estate/restaurant business. In the 1960s, my parents were friends with him. I was in high school then, and if he had a grand opening of a new restaurant, our family was invited. On the other side of the highway were a Whole Foods, a Bed Bath & Beyond, and several other stores, and part of a college campus, and the Boca Executive Airport was nearby as well.

Everybody I talked to tried to discourage me about buying the center because it was too big, but I liked the location and the condition of the buildings. The price tag was $60 million. Occupancy was at

97 percent, and though in Boston I was used to 100 percent, 97 was excellent in Florida, where all the properties I saw had vacancy factors in the 70s and 80s. It was risky deal for me, but I went through with it.

I was getting $22 to $25 per square foot, while the most expensive area listings go for $35 to $38 per square foot. But I'm going to keep up the building like it's an A-class building. The bathrooms were aged and needed to be redone. I didn't like the elevator area in the garage. It was dark and dingy, and I fixed that. I have seven or eight tenants with leases coming up and I want to get their prices up from $22 to $25 per square foot. Anybody at $25, maybe I'll raise them $25.50 at most. I want to keep them in the building. When I was at a celebratory lunch with the broker, he said, "Hey, you're 97 percent full," and I replied, "No, I'm 3 percent vacant. That's what matters to me."

Back in Boston in the 1960s, when I was working with my father, we were getting $110 for brand-new apartments per month on the first block of Marlboro Street. The key to our family's survival was making sure that those apartments were rented. Dad was more concerned about occupancy than getting every nickel out of every square foot. I learned that lesson from him. Take care of your building, and hang onto your tenants.

Ann and I had our first meeting with the leasing agents. They had a big billboard outside that said, "For Lease," with the name of the company and the telephone number. I said, "Hey, guys, you're not thinking. If I'm a small guy and I see these big, beautiful buildings and your fancy sign, I'm thinking I can't lease here. Or if some woman was driving by and her husband was starting a small consulting business, she'd think there was nothing for him here. We have some vacant space. Why not put up a sign saying, 'From 1,300 square feet'? Then the little guy will come look."

The agents put a sign in their window advertising smaller spaces, and now I'm 100 percent leased. The bottom line at the Peninsula Executive Center is that the leases are producing $1,850,000 a year, $1 million more than I was making at 7 Newbury Street. I am thankful for my Florida management team. They know what they're doing, and they're honorable. The handyman, Jon, had been working there ever since the place was built. I can identify with him. No mystery there. When I was young, I used to do his job.

If I were twenty-five and beginning my career, I'd start in Florida because of the tax savings. Even so, it's impossible for me give up on Boston. It's my hometown. It's in my blood. I got my experience in Back Bay, and I've seen the city grow. I'm in real estate more for the feeling of the accomplishment than for the money.

Still, I'm excited about all the possibilities in Florida. Ann and I formed a new company to handle our real estate. Best of all, I feel secure and peaceful.

# CHAPTER 26
# DOUBLE VISION

I never thought that the buildings I'd bought and sold would stand as the mileposts of my life. Of course, given my struggles in school as I was growing up, I never thought that I'd be buying, selling, owning, and managing so many properties. Yet there they stand, each one marking the passing of the years, leaving me with a rush of memories and the question of how I arrived where I am.

I've tried to answer that question in the earlier chapters of this memoir. Even so, it strikes me that I left out an essential—and private—part of my life, namely that ever since I started doing repairs for my father, I've had a double vision of myself.

On the one hand, I see a regular guy going about his business. The other vision is of a someone who looks at things differently and spots possibilities that others don't: an office building in an empty lot, for instance, or luxury condominiums instead of a dated, two-pump gas station. And because the people around you don't share your vision, you feel as if you are occupying a separate reality. Still, you believe in yourself, and because no one knows what you're dreaming, they don't disapprove of you and you're free to let your imagination roam. Once these possibilities become real and people see them and talk about them, they have no idea that you'd had that vision long before, and it would be—to my way of thinking—rude to tell them. And even if you tucked away your good manners for the moment and told them, it is unlikely that they would believe you, and in all likelihood they would dismiss the information as bragging.

So I lived quietly in my two worlds: the world I saw and the one I imagined.

To some degree, I inherited my double vision from my father. Dad would suggest an investment, and people would tell him that he didn't know what he was talking about. They were referring to his buying up old buildings that were expensive purchases for him—generally in the range of $100,000—and he'd often have to ask the seller to hold a second mortgage. His friends and some family members thought that he was gambling away his present by thinking too far into the future. Several of them said that he would be better off working for a company. It was, they said, safer to receive a paycheck every Friday and build up a pension for retirement than to speculate on distant, profitable days that might not ever arrive.

In that era, during the 1950s when I was a child, this was a standard, blue-collar attitude, and an understandable one. Some of his critics had come to the United States as penniless immigrants, and all of them had lived through the Great Depression, complete with memories of the unemployed waiting in bread lines and displaced families living in the shanties of Hoovervilles.

Dad gleaned different lessons from the Depression. First, if you're in your own business, you'll never be unemployed. And second, he saw the value in restoring buildings and creating an income stream, regardless of how modest, because eventually the mortgages on the buildings would be paid off and you would have more money to use in your personal life or to increase your portfolio of properties. And finally, this business didn't rely on you being in perfect health. He used to say that if you're a surgeon, you can make a great living, but if you injure your hands, you're in trouble. Thus, because your mind is the last to go, you should you use your mind to make money, not your hands.

My father preached this philosophy to anyone who would listen. One willing listener was me. Another was Yohaness Salou, an immigrant from Ethiopia. Yohaness was an attendant at a lot on the southwest corner of Newbury Street where my father used to park. Yohaness would station himself in a four-foot-by-four-foot shack with a coal-burning potbelly stove to keep warm in the winter. Dad was always a one-on-one person, and he loved talking real estate. He began talking to Yohaness about it.

Soon enough, Yohaness was considering buying a two-family house in Cambridge, and my father helped him buy it. I would always smile and say hello to Yohaness when I parked there, but he had a special relationship with my father. As time went on, with Dad's expertise and financing, Yohaness began buying and selling rental properties, and today he is a multimillionaire. He told me that Dad was a father figure to him, and he feels as though we are brothers. It is a feeling I return. Dad identified with hardworking people on the way up, and he frequently tried to help them. But he was quiet about it. Eight hundred people attended his wake, and his two sisters sat in the funeral parlor looking at each other. One of them said, "We didn't really know our brother."

I knew him though, and like Dad, I identify with hard workers on the rise. I've tried to help my small tenants by tailoring deals to their needs.

As for the naysayers who disagreed with my father when he was starting in real estate—long after he was gone, I'd run into them now and again and they'd tell me, "I should've listened to your father and bought some property."

Early on, I knew that I'd need my double vision, that I would have to think differently. I learned that in school by being a dreadful student. Nonetheless, I was aware that I had some talent for fixing things and the discipline to work hard, and because I became accustomed to people not believing in me, I developed an attitude that one day I would show what I could do—a motivation that has stayed with me. I also learned, when I was in college, that there were predictors of success other than stellar grades.

One afternoon, I had to drive to my prep school in Bristol, Connecticut, to retrieve a transcript so I could transfer, once again, to another college. I saw the dean, and we started talking. When he told me that the best student in my class had dropped out of college and was working in a filling station, I said, "Well, at least I'm still trying."

And I am trying still. Later on in my career, I'd repeatedly see graduates of highly respected universities struggle in the real estate business, and I realized that one great advantage I had when I started out in the business was that I'd lived a blue-collar life and had developed a white-collar mindset. It was the reason I got along so well with my workers. In my soul, I'm one of them. My imagination is the difference.

My maternal grandfather Nishan, who owned the Fresh Pond Market in Cambridge, used to tell me a story about the market across the street from his place. One day, a customer came in and said, "The sign in your window says it's $4 a pound for strawberries. But the guy across the street has a sign saying that he's got strawberries for $1.99 a pound."

My grandfather asked, "Why didn't you buy them across the street?"

"Because he ran out of strawberries," the customer explained.

"Well," my grandfather replied, "when I run out of strawberries, I'll change my sign to $1.99 a pound."

That story still makes me smile. In fact, I often think about it because for me the story represents the common sense that enabled millions of immigrants to America to climb the socioeconomic ladder. In addition, I always felt a kinship to the generations that produced my grandparents and parents. They struck me as so grateful for what they had, and I'm not only talking about those who achieved my father's level of success. I'm talking about all those regular Joes who had decent jobs and a house and enough money to take a vacation and ultimately retire without the fear of going hungry. They had come through the Depression and world wars, and they understood that their security was achievement enough.

I hardly grew up in the lap of luxury, though I knew that I'd never go hungry. Much later, when my wife Jane died so young, I discovered how it felt in life to hold the short end of the stick. So I'm grateful for what I've accomplished, particularly because I did it on my own, with my double vision. I look at where I came from and where I am now. It was a lot of hard work. I get tired thinking about it, and of course I'm aware that lots of people work hard and success eludes them.

I've been lucky in business but luckiest in my personal life. Jane's cousin, Michael, told me some time ago that I had gotten lucky twice—once with Jane and now with Ann. And Michael added that I had the good fortune to have my son Chris, who helped me through the loss of his mother and who has brought me a whole new round of joy with his wife, Noel, and my granddaughters, Celina, Charlie, and Chloe

Yet even though I've reached the age where one concerns oneself more with estate planning than new projects, I still find myself hiring new office staff and thinking that with some effort I could double the size of my business in six years.

I'm not sure I'll try that, but I do know that while I'm here, I will never stop imagining.

Hotel Armenia in the capital city of Yerevan. My sister Gail belonged to some groups that were trying to help Armenia recover from its Soviet past. I asked my accountant if I could afford to lose a million dollars. He said yes, so I asked my mother if she thought we should invest in the hotel. She liked what Gail was doing, and in the end, as a family, we invested with three other investors.

250 Boylston Street, Boston. It was a retail condo, and when I heard a tenant wanted to lease the space, I bought it. One of the easiest transactions of my career. My advice—it's good to buy a building that has a tenant.

75 Newbury Street, Boston.

137 Newbury Street, Boston.

129 Commonwealth Avenue, Boston. Jane, Chris, and I would live here. The renovation, which lasted for fourteen months, became a labor of love for me, and today, twenty-six years later, I still marvel at how the house turned out. I understand that talking about it I can begin to sound as tiresome as a parent bragging about a child. For me, though, this goes beyond the pride of creation or ownership. Buildings, to me, are art. I get the same aesthetic pleasure looking at them as the aficionados who ooh and aah at the paintings in the Museum of Fine Arts.

168 Newbury Street, Boston.

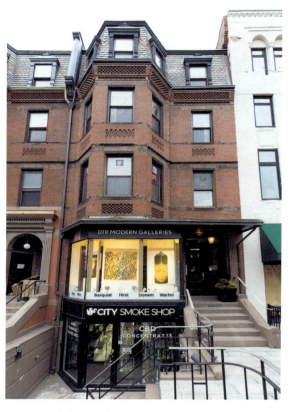

167 Newbury Street, Boston.

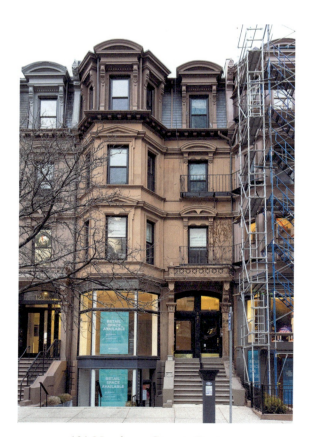

121 Newbury Street, Boston.

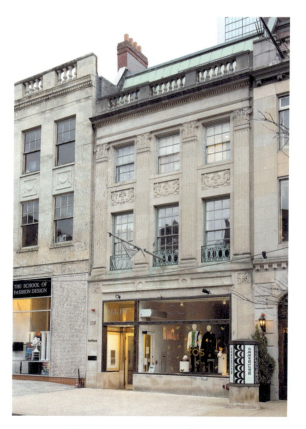

138 Newbury Street, Boston.

244 Newbury Street, Boston.

7 Newbury Street, Boston.

11 Newbury Street, Boston.

South Cape Village, Mashpee, Mass. I'd been through the approval process with the Back Bay Commission in Boston, which was about as pleasurable as a double root canal. Believe it not, the Cape Cod Commission was worse—like having all your teeth pulled without Novocain.

On September 7, 2014, Ann and I had a Jewish-Armenian wedding at the Four Seasons Hotel in Boston.

Great Exhuma, the Bahamas. I started building this place in 2003 to distract myself from Jane's illness. I finally moved in 2006 and sold it in 2020. It was the worst real-estate I ever made.

132 South Bay Road, Osterville, Mass. The center house is the dream home I built on the Cape.

141 West Key Palm Road, Boca Raton, Florida. Ann and I have lived here since 2015.

300 Cambridge Street, Boston. In 1998, I purchased this site. A gas station stood on it, along with a zip car lot and Mexican restaurant. When the leases ended in 2016, I put up this building.

Four Generations. Top row (L to R): Me, Ann, my daughter-in-law Noel, and Chris. Bottom row (L to R): My granddaughter, Celina, brother-in-law Richard O'Reilly, Mom, my sister Gail, and my granddaughter, Charlie.

Peninsula Executive Center, two buildings with a four-story aboveground garage and beautiful landscaping. The center was part of an office park, convenient for people commuting to work. What I liked about it most was that it was on Glades Road, so it had its own exit on the highway, and it was right down the street from Town Center, one of the area's largest malls, and I noticed that even during tough times, the mall was upping its game.

Printed in the United States
by Baker & Taylor Publisher Services